The Fifth Beginning

The Fifth Beginning

What Six Million Years of Human
History Can Tell Us about Our Future

Robert L. Kelly

UNIVERSITY OF CALIFORNIA PRESS

University of California Press, one of the most
distinguished university presses in the United States,
enriches lives around the world by advancing scholarship
in the humanities, social sciences, and natural sciences. Its
activities are supported by the UC Press Foundation and
by philanthropic contributions from individuals and
institutions. For more information, visit www.ucpress.edu.

University of California Press
Oakland, California

© 2016 by Robert L. Kelly

Library of Congress Cataloging-in-Publication Data

Names: Kelly, Robert L., author.
Title: The fifth beginning : what six million years of
   human history can tell us about our future /
   Robert L. Kelly.
Description: Oakland, California : University of
   California Press, [2016] | Includes bibliographical
   references and index.
Identifiers: LCCN 2016012935 | ISBN 9780520293120
   (cloth : alk. paper) | ISBN 9780520966369 (ebook)
Subjects: LCSH: Civilization. | Culture. | Social history.
Classification: LCC CB69 .K44 2016 | DDC 909—dc23
LC record available at http://lccn.loc.gov/2016012935

Manufactured in the United States of America

25 24 23 22 21 20 19 18 17 16

10 9 8 7 6 5 4 3 2 1

For my father, an optimistic man

Contents

Preface

I think of myself as a "dirt archaeologist." I like nothing better than sur-
veying the mountains for sites or digging in the dirt for scraps of bone and
broken arrowheads. I've done exactly that for the last forty-three years,
and I still look forward to my time "in the field" each summer. Like most
archaeologists, I do archaeology because I enjoy being dirty, crouching in
an excavation in the baking sun, bathing in glacial mountain streams, and
mapping a site in a cold, driving rain. Also, like most archaeologists, I do
archaeology because of a deep need to understand human history.

Ask archaeologists to justify what they do for a living, and they will
say that they study the past in order to know the future. Unfortunately,
few of us do more than pay lip service to that claim. I decided it was
time for me to do more than that; the result is the book before you.

I don't intend to use prehistory to predict the future, to foretell what
is coming so that I can get ahead of the curve. Instead, I want to understand the past so that I can help *create* the future. I suppose becoming a
father had something to do with that; I care about the world my sons
will inhabit. However, I'm not a politician and never will be, so I won't
create the future by running for office. Nor am I in a financial position
to put wealth toward a good cause. And I'm not an economist who
might tell us how to structure an economy so that folks at the bottom
don't get hurt. No, I'm just a dirt archaeologist. So I use what I know,
prehistory, and this book is my small contribution toward making the
world a better place for future generations.

That last sentence will strike many as silly, even Pollyannaish. Naively, in the early twentieth century some people believed humanity was on the verge of world peace. Then World War I hit. "Serves us right," I'm sure some people thought. "We let our guard down, and we got tank and gas warfare." Our attitude toward the future has gone downhill ever since. Some days it does seem as though there's no reason, none at all, to be hopeful. But I choose to remain hopeful, because if I don't—if we don't—then surely the world will go to hell. I'm frankly not an optimistic person, but I am a practical one. So I choose the attitude that will lead to the result we all seek.

I also choose to keep this book short and sweet and, in places, lighthearted. It's not that I don't take prehistory seriously, to say nothing of the world's future. In fact, it's precisely because I take both seriously that I wanted to write a book people might actually read. If you want a long, somber recitation of all the stuff that's going to hit the fan in the coming years, there are plenty of other books. I'll focus on what humanity could do right, rather than on what humanity has done wrong.

Some of my colleagues will quibble about how I've chosen to present prehistory, and they may not like all the details and alternative perspectives that I've left aside. I apologize in advance to them, but I've got to tell the story as I've come to understand it. And I focus on the big picture because I think that's archaeology's greatest contribution.

. . .

This book began as a lecture at Washington State University in 2007 at the invitation of the Department of Anthropology. I appreciate the patience of the audience who had to hear the first, unformed version of these ideas. I developed the ideas in additional lectures at the Universities of Arizona, Colorado, Nevada, and Wyoming. Again, I appreciate the opportunities those lectures gave me to think more about this subject.

I began writing the book while on sabbatical leave at St. John's College at the University of Cambridge in the fall of 2012. I appreciate the office space that St. John's gave me (especially since it overlooked the Master's Garden) and conversations with Robert Hinde and an old friend, Nick James. I also thank James Ahern, Mark Heinz, Stephen Lekson, Lin Poyer, Rachel Reckin, Torben Rick, Lynne Schepartz, and Carla Sinopoli for providing comments on earlier drafts; Lenore Hart for helping me write a prospectus; University of California Press editor Reed Malcolm for taking a chance on the book; and copy editor Barbara Armentrout. There are too many to list here, but I also thank my many colleagues who kindly answered questions over the past several years as I worked on the manuscript. All mistakes, of course, are mine alone.

My career as an archaeologist has given me the opportunity to travel around the world. Those travels gave me a perspective that was crucial to this book's completion. And I couldn't have made those travels, and I couldn't have written this book, without Lin Poyer—friend, confidante, critic, and wife. Thank you. Where shall we go now?

Robert L. Kelly
Laramie, Wyoming
May, 2016

CHAPTER I

The End of the World as We Know It

I have seen yesterday. I know tomorrow.

—Inscription in Tutankhamun's tomb

"My father," the elderly woman said quietly, "was born in slavery."

In the 1980s, when I was teaching anthropology at the University of Louisville, I gave a lecture using archaeology to peer into the future. I tried to be optimistic and thought I had succeeded, but a student in the front row raised his hand and said dejectedly, "The way things have been is the way things always will be." I was struggling for an answer when an elderly African American woman came to my rescue. I knew this woman because she frequently stayed after class to chat. I knew that she had been born in 1905; that she had had no chance for an education early in life; and that she had seen to her children's and grandchildren's education before deciding it was time for her own. But I clearly didn't know everything about her.

As she spoke, students turned and looked at the woman, as if seeing her for the first time. None had ever been so close to the heinous institution of slavery. She explained that her father had been born just before the Emancipation Proclamation and had married late in life. He had lived through Reconstruction, and she had lived through the Jim Crow era, KKK lynchings, Selma, and the civil rights movement. "Things do change," she concluded.

Yet the pessimistic student dismissed her with a wave of his hand. It was rude, but it wasn't rudeness he intended to signal; it was hopelessness.

You've heard the joke that the light at the end of the tunnel is an oncoming train. That's how many people see the future—a locomotive bearing down upon them and no place to jump off the tracks. And why not? Climate change, economic inequality, crowded cities, global pollution, terrorism, corrupt political systems, random shootings, and atrocities in the name of religion leave little room for hope. Many people today feel their lives are a never-ending episode of *The Walking Dead,* zombies lurking around every corner.

But there is reason for hope, and the economist Herbert Stein tells us why in his famous "law": if something can't go on forever, it won't. As an archaeologist, I know that world prehistory proves Stein's law. Even a quick glance at the ancient world tells us the past was quite different from the present. Fifteen thousand years ago, everyone in the world was a hunter-gatherer; today, almost no one is. Few people are even farmers; in fact, only a tiny fraction of the world's population is directly involved in food production. Our Stone Age ancestors could not have envisioned our sophisticated technology or global economy. Yes, things do change.

But I can hear you saying, "OK, the way things are is not the way things were, but maybe the way things are is the way things will be from now on. Maybe we've reached the end of history."

Maybe, but I doubt it. I doubt it because understanding why humanity changed in the past helps us understand why the future will be different from today. In fact, an understanding of prehistory leads me to conclude that we can expect everything from technology to politics to international order—even the very character of humanity—to change radically in the near future.

And now I can hear you saying, "Everything's going to change all right. We're all going to hell in a handbasket!"

I can't shut the door on that possibility, but I don't think that's the lesson to draw from six million years of human evolution.

From the perspective of a species, evolution's job is to ensure the continuation of that species' genetic material. As long as you live to reproduce and rear young to reproduce, evolution doesn't care about you. It has no greater purpose. What's curious about the process, though, is that in achieving its purpose, evolution creates some creatures remarkably different from those it started with. Mammals are the products of single-celled organisms that fought microscopic battles in the primordial seas hundreds of millions of years ago. Those songbirds singing sweetly on your back fence came from fearsome dinosaurs (think about that next time you munch on chicken nuggets). And everyone today—from Dutch dairy farmers to Silicon Valley computer scientists—is the result of our ancestors trying to be the best hunter-gatherers they could be. In trying to be one thing, organisms reach a tipping point and become something completely different. This is what evolutionary theorists label *emergent phenomena.*

In this book I argue that humans have passed through four such tipping points over the past six million years. I label them *beginnings* since they mark periods when the basic character of human existence changed and our species began a new life. In chronological order these are the beginning of technology, the beginning of culture, the beginning of agriculture, and the beginning of a political organization called the *state.* Knowing how archaeologists recognize these beginnings will lead to the conclusion that we've arrived at yet another tipping point: the fifth beginning.

Humans arrived at each of these beginnings through several processes, but a primary driver is increased competition brought about by population growth. If you know nothing else about evolution, you probably know the expression "survival of the fittest." It's often attributed to Darwin, although he didn't coin it (that was his contemporary, Herbert Spencer; Darwin did use it in later editions of *On the Origin of Species*). Evolution does indeed thrive on competition; it's the "red in tooth and claw" part of it (Darwin didn't say that either; that's from Alfred Lord Tennyson's 1850 poem *In Memoriam A.H.H.*). Competition secures the necessities of life by securing an organism's advantage over others, by being better at finding food, shelter, or mates. As we will see in subsequent chapters, our Pleistocene ancestors who wielded stone tools beat out those who didn't. Those who had gained the capacity for culture beat out those who did not. Agriculturalists eventually overran hunter-gatherers. And chiefdoms and tribes gave way to state societies, which now dominate the world.

Despite the power of competition, those who study evolution are aware that altruism and cooperation are also essential components of the evolutionary process.[1] They help produce alliances, and alliances—mutually beneficial, you-scratch-my-back-and-I'll-scratch-yours relationships—are often integral to competition. In the fifth beginning, the one we are now in, I expect the evolutionary process to encourage more such relationships and to bring about an economic, social, and political order based more on cooperation than on competition; in fact, the fifth beginning might mark an era in which we compete at cooperation.

In my mind, the only question is whether we make this transition, the fifth beginning, the easy way or the hard way.

. . .

I'm sure there was a time when I wanted to be a cowboy, or a fireman, or an astronaut, but I can't recall wanting to be anything other than an archaeologist. As a boy, I loved the outdoors, camping, and the idea of living off the land. That led me to an interest in Native Americans and in how they used to live. I read what I could, searched for caves, and collected arrowheads from the fields of a neighboring dairy farmer. Anything old fascinated me, so I tracked down colonial roads from old maps, explored the crumbled foundations of abandoned mills, and raked through historic dumps for bottles. I filled my bedroom with arrowheads, bones, and fossils. Fortunately, my parents indulged this hobby and when I was eleven or twelve years old, my mother gave me a copy of Sir Leonard Woolley's 1961 book *The Young Archaeologist;* it still sits on my university desk. You might think this an odd childhood, but actually many professional archaeologists found their passion at a young age.

National Geographic captivated me, especially its articles about "primitive" people in far-off places and those about Jane Goodall and her chimpanzees. The magazine led me to the work of Louis and Mary Leakey, who, at the time, were discovering the remains of early human ancestors in eastern Africa. I yearned to be there, in Olduvai Gorge, walking those barren hillsides looking for tiny scraps of bone. Although I grew up in rural New England, my heart has always been in windswept deserts and mountains.

In 1973, when I was sixteen, a thoughtful high school guidance counselor showed me a brochure for Educational Expeditions International (EEI); today it's known as Earthwatch. This group matches interested volunteers with field scientists such as geologists, biologists, zoologists, and archaeologists. EEI gave scholarships for high school students to spend a summer working on a research project. I applied for and received one, and was sent to work with David Hurst Thomas, an archaeologist at the American Museum of Natural History. It was my good fortune to have crossed paths with a rising star. I worked with David as he excavated a cave in central Nevada and for years afterwards until, in fact, I began my own doctoral field research. Today, he and I coauthor two college textbooks.

Over the past forty-odd years, I've participated in field projects throughout the western United States, as well as in the U.S. southeast, New York City (where I helped excavate a site on Wall Street), Maine, and Kentucky. I've worked on an Inca site on the edge of Chile's Atacama Desert. I've excavated 13,000-year-old "Paleo-Indian" campsites, nineteenth-century privies, human burials, pueblos, and caves—in deserts and humid forests, on coasts and 12,000-foot mountain peaks.

I've also done ethnographic research in Madagascar with the Mikea, a group of horticulturalist/hunter-gatherers.

Through all of this I remained interested in hunter-gatherers. I admit that my initial attraction was romantic. There was something very earthy and genuine about people who live simply, using their ingenuity and effort to harvest what nature provides and leaving only a small footprint behind. It seemed to me that hunter-gatherers were closest to how humans should live: peacefully, in small groups, with few material possessions.

Of course, like most of the things we believe as youths, this was partly an illusion. Hunter-gatherers can be violent and territorial—and materialistic: one young Mikea man asked me to bring him "an airplane, or maybe a tractor," and another asked me for everything I had, right down to my wedding ring. Many hunter-gatherers hunted species to extinction, and others altered their landscape's vegetation by periodically burning it off. When one Mikea man left the savanna burning behind us, I asked him why he had done so. He looked at me with surprise and replied: "It'll be easier to walk through when we return." (He was right.)

Humanity has spent 99 percent of its existence as hunter-gatherers; it was an enormously successful adaptation. Consequently, I can't study hunter-gatherers without also thinking about what early human life was like and how we came to be the species we are. And that led me to wonder why we changed, why we became agriculturalists and why we developed cities, armies, slavery, and ruling classes. If a simple technology coupled with life in small egalitarian, nomadic groups worked so well for so long, why did we give it up? Why aren't we still hunter-gatherers?

. . .

Archaeologists devote their lives to looking backward, to seeing where humanity has been. That might seem to be an odd qualification for someone who wants to write about the future. But I hope to show you that archaeology is not just about the dead; it's also about the living. And it's not just about the past; it's also about the future.

Archaeology provides a crucial record of human history. For most of our history, it's the only record we have. Yet if you read a book on world history, you'll most likely find prehistory covered only in the first chapter or perhaps only in that chapter's first paragraphs. In textbooks, history often begins with the Egyptian, Greek, Roman, and Chinese "civilizations." Prehistory is mere stage setting: *you got your apes, some come down from the trees and walk upright, our brains get bigger, we make stone tools, paint cave art, grow wheat*—and then on to the real history, the important stuff. But by relegating prehistory to background, historians miss the big picture.

Archaeologists are amused when they hear hyperbole like "He's the best football player in history" or "This motion picture is the biggest blockbuster of all time." American football and motion pictures both trace their origins to the 1890s—just over a century ago. To an archaeologist, that's less than the proverbial blink of an eye. We think in time scales of thousands, tens of thousands, or hundreds of thousands of years. I admit those timescales are difficult to imagine. And yet, if we want to understand significant beginnings in human history—not just the small tweaks that written history records but big, top-to-bottom, front-to-back, no-turning-back kinds of change—we need to look at human history using the biggest scale possible, one provided only by archaeology.

So why do archaeologists think humanity took the particular course that it did, passing through several new beginnings? Here's a hint: it has nothing to do with progress. Instead, evolution has always tried to make us the best at one thing, but in doing so, it turned us into something quite different. My cherished hunter-gatherers, for example, became agriculturalists while trying to be the best hunter-gatherers they could be. And in trying to be the best industrial, capitalist, competitive nation-states we can be, we too should expect to become something completely different. To cut to the chase, capitalism, the globalization of culture, and the arms race are working together to guarantee a complete change in the organization of human society. It's the end of war as a viable way to resolve disputes, the end of the nation-state and capitalism as sacred organizational and economic forms, and the beginning of global citizenship. It's the end of the world as we know it.

. . .

As the ball dropped on Times Square on December 31, 1999, many people expected chaos to reign as computer clocks tripped over to 2000 (never mind that they had already tripped over in Beijing and London without consequence). Some computers were not designed to change the fourth-place digit from 1 to 2, and many expected failures in everything from airline equipment to banking systems. But the hype did not live up to expectations. Planes did not fall from the sky, and the world's financial system did not collapse.

True believers, however, were undeterred and they looked elsewhere for confirmation that the world was ending. Some found it in the traditions of the Maya, who, the story goes, predicted the world would end on December 21, 2012.

Since you are reading this book, you know that prediction didn't come true. But don't blame the Maya for being Chicken Littles, because they never actually predicted the end of the world. The Maya were pre-occupied with time, and they worked with several calendars that told them when the king had to perform a lot of world-renewing ceremonials, rites that often involved his blood (sometimes drawn from his tongue with obsidian blades—it's not always good to be king).

One Maya calendar in particular bothered the modern doomsayers, the Long Count. The Long Count literally counts the number of days since the beginning of time, or what the Maya considered the beginning of time. Since the Maya were so good about putting dates on things, scholars with code-breaking skills comparable to those of Alan Turing were able to reckon the Long Count with the Gregorian calendar and calculate the Maya beginning of time and of the Long Count: August 11, 3114 B.C. The Long Count is made in five units of days: b'ak'tun (144,000 days), k'atun (7,200 days), tun (360 days), winal (20 days), and k'in (1 day). Mayanists write dates with shorthand, for example, 12.2.6.4.2, which is 12 b'ak'tun (12 × 144,000 = 1,728,000 days), 2 k'atun (2 × 7,200 = 14,400 days), and so on. Add these figures together and you have the number of days that have passed since August 11, 3114 B.C. With this information, archaeologists can date events in Maya history with remarkable precision.

The problem comes from the fact that on December 21, 2012, the Maya Long Count clicked over to 13.0.0.0.0. I guess this seemed ominous to some members of a culture that stigmatizes the number 13. But it didn't bother the Maya (13 was a special number to them, but so was 20). In fact, as far as we know, they mentioned the future date only twice, both in harmless ways. All the hype and hoopla had no basis in Maya calendrics.[2]

The Maya did not predict the end of the world, but many other people have done so. One wave of millennial movements in the United States arose in the early nineteenth century, when a variety of new religions sprang up claiming the second coming of Christ and the apocalypse. The Mormon faith (the Church of Jesus Christ of Latter-day Saints) arose in the 1820s, as did a number of utopian communities, such as New Harmony, Indiana (1825). The Shakers (more properly known as the United Society of Believers in Christ's Second Appearing) formed in England in the mid-eighteenth century, but reached their greatest numbers in the United States about 1840.

These phenomena are known to anthropologists as "revitalization movements." In such movements a prophet claims that the end of the world's current order is imminent. Those prophets assert that people have lost their way, and to survive the coming apocalypse, they must return to their roots, a process that, oddly, almost always entails new beliefs. Shakers, for example, shunned sex, believing it to be the root of all evil and no longer necessary in a world about to end. The Mormon faith added a new chapter to the Bible, one that describes Jesus's appearance in the New World for a time after his resurrection.

Obviously, the world didn't end in the 1840s, but that didn't stop people from thinking Armageddon was just around the next corner. In fact, it seems every generation thinks it's living in end-days. The current round of end-of-the-world fever was anticipated by the rock band R.E.M., with their 1987 hit "The End of the World as We Know It (And I Feel Fine)." But it wasn't only rock stars who had a sense of impending doom. "The End is Near" is normally associated with cartoons of a placard-carrying ascetic. But starting in the late 1980s, a parade of respectable authors titled their works with the same sense of finality. The first was Bill McKibben's 1989 book, *The End of Nature*. The same year Francis Fukuyama published an article (in *The National Interest*) entitled "The End of History?" which appeared as a book in 1992. In fact, there are about twenty books with titles asserting the end of one thing or another.[3]

Using "The End of" in a title is clearly a marketing ploy aimed at the mystique that surrounded the end of the twentieth century. These books aren't religious tracts, but they are nonetheless "millennial" books that describe end-times. And while some are upbeat (who can't applaud the end of racism, poverty, war, or, especially, of politics?), many tell us that tragedies, all of our own devising, are fast approaching and that we must reform ourselves quickly to avoid them. Other authors (such as Jared Diamond in *The World until Yesterday*) avoided the end-of-the-world marketing shtick but still proclaimed that human evolution did not design us for life in large cities; diets high in fats, sugars, or carbohydrates (turns out that nothing you eat is good for you); or for cooperation on the scale we now need. Biologist E.O. Wilson has issued similar warnings for years (e.g., in *The Future of Life, The Social Conquest of Earth,* and *The Meaning of Human Existence*).[4] Take a look in any bookstore and you'll see many nonfiction best sellers are pessimistic—and with good reason.[5]

Although we have made remarkable technological progress in just the past century, the daily headlines of mayhem and atrocities lead many to see the glass as half-empty. Vice President Al Gore presented a litany of interconnected problems facing humanity in *The Future,* and Henry Kissinger warned of coming chaos in *World Order.* In *The Ends of the Earth* Robert Kaplan sees little hope for much of Africa and Asia, with so many of their countries wracked by disease, failed governments, warlords, crime, and environmental destruction.[6] Since 1980 inequality both within and between countries has increased dramatically. In fact, Oxfam estimates that the richest 62 people in the world today control as much wealth as the poorest 3.5 *billion* of the world's population.[7] Even if that estimate is off by one or two orders of magnitude (maybe it's 620 or 6,200 people), the statistic would still be alarming.[8]

And that's not all. Elizabeth Kolbert (*The Sixth Extinction*), Naomi Klein (*This Changes Everything*), Gaia Vince (*Adventures in the Anthropocene*), Alan Weisman (*Countdown*), Julian Cribb (*The Coming Famine*), and Naomi Oreskes and Erik M. Conway (*The Collapse of Western Civilization: A View from the Future*) all expect population growth and climate change to bring horrendous problems. In fact, we may have already passed the Rubicon of climate change and can hope only to respond to its effects rather than prevent them.[9] The current human population of almost seven and a half billion is expected to reach nine to ten billion before the end of this century—in a world that some demographers estimate can maintain a first-world lifestyle for everyone with minimal environmental damage at a population of only one and a half billion.[10] Someone is going to lose.

Sadly, most of these authors doubt whether we have the collective will to implement the necessary solutions as quickly as they are needed. Instead, they believe our political and economic systems guarantee that nothing short of a combined environmental, demographic, economic, and political catastrophe will produce change.

Others, though, are optimistic. In the glass-is-half-full category are Robert Wright in *Non-Zero: The Logic of Human Destiny,* Matt Ridley in *The Rational Optimist,* Steven Pinker in *The Better Angels of Our Nature,* Charles Kenny in *Getting Better,* Joshua Goldstein in *Winning the War on War,* and Angus Deaton in *The Great Escape: Health, Wealth, and the Origins of Inequality.* These authors point to more promising statistics: All forms of violence are down (even as our perception of violence is up). Food availability is up (though malnutrition and obesity are worse). Child mortality is down, and life expectancy has risen by 50 percent in the past century. Since 1980 the proportion of the world's population that lives on $1 a day is down from 42 to 14 percent. Advances in medicine are remarkable, and life spans have increased by some thirty years in developed nations. Globalization opens more doors and opportunities than ever before. The Internet has made the exchange of ideas among a global population possible, and that creates knowledge at a rate the world has never seen. The remarkable ability of our species for cleverness leads Diane Ackerman, in *The Human Age*, to see hope for resolving environmental problems. If we've got a ways to go, and we do, at least some indicators are moving in the right direction.[11]

Prehistory teaches us that humans excel at solving problems, that evolution has always been remaking us. Of course, as stockbrokers say, past performance is no guarantee of future results. We could indeed be headed to hell in a handbasket. But prehistory tells me that doesn't have to be the case; the future could be ours to make.

Before we can get to the future, however, we must examine the past. And before we can do that, we need to know a little about how archaeologists think in order to show how they recognize humanity's significant beginnings, beginnings that have repeatedly marked the end of the world as we know it.

CHAPTER 2

How Archaeologists Think

It's not what you find, it's what you find out.

—Archaeologist David Hurst Thomas

Some years ago I was sitting on the curb in Truth or Consequences, New Mexico. The town once called itself Hot Springs but changed its name in 1950 when the host of a popular radio program promised to broadcast the show from the first town to adopt the program's name. So T or C, as it's commonly known, is a town with a sense of humor. And on the day that I found myself sitting along the roadside, I could see that humor reflected in the residents' bumper stickers. Hard-core *Star Trek* fans will see it in "My God, Jim, he's dead. You get his wallet, I'll get his tricorder." And the one that rang true for me was this: "Archaeologists are the cowboys of science."

Cowboys and archaeologists like to have fun. I remember the 1976 Fourth of July in Austin, Nevada, another small town with a sense of humor. Our crew was enjoying the holiday at a little dive affectionately named the "Austin Hilton," when Les Boyd, a cowboy from the Triple T ranch, rode his horse into the doorway and challenged "any SOB in here" to a horse race. No one seemed to think this odd, and when someone took his bet, Les turned his horse and clumped out. Austin's entire population (it's a very small town) migrated out to the town's dirt airstrip. Someone fired a pistol and the race was on. Boyd was an excellent horseman, and he galloped full tilt down the runway. Holding the reins in the crook of his elbow, and with a mug of beer in one hand and a lit cigar in the other, he turned in the saddle and taunted his challenger, "Come on! Come on!"

Archaeologists are a lot like that. Excavating a fragile piece of bone with a dental tool under the hot sun can be tedious, if not damned irritating, so archaeologists make it not only bearable but memorable with stories and jokes. I've heard entire episodes of *The Simpsons* on excavations and snippets of student conversations that leave me wondering what they are talking about, things like "Oh yeah? Well, Chuck Norris has counted to infinity, twice," or my favorite, "Let me tell you, that was one constipated monkey." While eating lunch one especially hot day in Nevada, a student declared, "Oranges are better than sex!" and initiated a long discussion of things to do with fruit. I can't repeat it here.

Archaeologists need a sense of humor. Archaeology isn't rocket science; in fact, it's harder. At least rocket scientists know whether their ideas are wrong: the rocket goes up or it doesn't. But without a time machine, archaeologists can't be certain whether we're right. We constantly improve our methods, but we have to admit that anytime we say, "Here's what happened in the past," we are actually saying, "Here's what we think happened, at such-and-such level of probability." (We don't actually say that because, frankly, it would be boring.)

. . .

But sometimes we *can* interpret the past with detail that astonishes even us. For example, in 1991, hikers discovered the naked body of a man high in the Italian Alps; the body was so well-preserved that they assumed it was of a recently deceased hiker. They called in the local authorities, who began recovery efforts. But the team soon suspected that the body, frozen in the ice and snow, was not recent. Radiocarbon dating eventually verified that hunch, showing that the man, now known as Ötzi, died some 5,100 years ago, during Europe's late Neolithic (the "New Stone Age," from 9,000 to 4,000 years ago).

Ötzi's body was so well-preserved that his fifty tattoos are still visible. From analyses of the skeleton we know that he was about forty-five years old when he died, stood five feet tall, and weighed 110 pounds. He had dark, wavy, shoulder-length hair and a beard. His teeth were heavily worn from a diet high in stone-ground wheat, but he had few cavities. The high arsenic content of his hair suggests he had recently spent time around copper smelting, and growth-arrest lines in his fingernails tell us he had been ill eight, thirteen, and sixteen weeks prior to his death—probably as a result of a chronic condition. His DNA tells us he had brown eyes, was lactose intolerant, had type O blood, was related to modern-day Sardinians, and probably had Lyme disease. Using the same methods that forensic scientists employ to reconstruct faces from skulls, Italian researchers created a portrait of Ötzi. It's the only Neolithic face our world has ever seen.[1]

We also know what Ötzi carried and wore. His shoes were fashioned from deerskin and bearskin, stuffed with grass. His leggings, loincloth, and coat were made of domesticated goatskin, and he carried a woven grass mat and wore a bearskin cap. His coat was fastened with a belt of calf leather, in which Ötzi carried several stone tools, along with dried fungus as fire tinder. He had an unfinished longbow fashioned from yew wood and covered in blood (as water repellent), as well as a stone knife with an ash-wood handle tucked in a fiber sheath. He carried an antler-tipped, wooden-handled tool for flaking stone and a quiver of chamois hide, which contained two complete and twelve incomplete arrows. Judging from the way the fletching was tied, one of the complete arrows was made by a right-handed person and the other by a left-handed one. He also carried a hazel-wood backpack frame, a net of bark fiber, and two birch-bark containers, one carrying fresh maple leaves and, at one time, coals from which to kindle a fire. No doubt his prized possession was his ax of yew wood, with a sharp copper head hafted to the handle with birch tar and leather binding. Copper was rare in the Neolithic, so the ax indicates Ötzi's status.

The composition of Ötzi's teeth and bones tell us that he grew up in the upper Eisack Valley of the Alps, and that he had lived for the last ten years in the Vinschgau Valley, which was the geologic source of his stone tools. From analysis of his intestinal contents, we know that he ate a last meal of unleavened wheat bread, deer, wild goat meat, and some greens. The pollen in his lungs suggests he was in the Vinschgau in the twelve hours before he died, and the pollen and chlorophyll content of the maple leaves tell us he made his last journey in June.

And we know how Ötzi died: murdered, shot in the back by an arrow and then possibly struck on the head. X-ray examination found the stone point, which had pierced his left shoulder blade and a major blood vessel. Ötzi would have bled out in minutes. He also had a cut on his forehead and cut marks on his fingers, possibly defensive wounds from warding off the blows of a knife. Several of his right ribs bore evidence of healed breaks, but several of his left ribs were broken shortly before he died.

Despite his body being over five thousand years old, we know the story of Ötzi's last day on earth. He left his home in the Vinschgau Valley in June; he was unhurried, for he packed things he would need for a journey of several days. Someone tracked him, or encountered him. They fought, and Ötzi escaped, but his assailant caught him near the mountain crest and killed him with a single arrow to the back. I'd guess that the assailant was an experienced archer, rather than just lucky, and thus he was probably a male of Ötzi's age. And I'd guess the killer was in fact someone who knew Ötzi well. Why? The killer would have seen Ötzi fall, since such a well-placed shot could not have come from more than fifteen meters away. Perhaps the killer stood over Ötzi, waiting for him to take his last breath. And yet he left Ötzi's belongings behind, including his valuable copper-headed ax. Why leave such booty? My guess is he couldn't use it because he was a member of Ötzi's own village, possibly someone who bore a grudge. If he had brought the ax home, others would have recognized it and asked questions.

If we had a time machine, we could almost certainly go back to the Neolithic and convict Ötzi's killer.

. . .

This kind of detailed, forensic approach is what interests the public about archaeology. And why not? It makes for great reading because the details give us a sense that "we are there." It connects us to the past on a personal level. We find it easier to understand things when they are put in terms that make sense to us as individuals. Few people read sociological journal articles filled with statistics on marital infidelity, but politicians' peccadilloes make front page news.

Archaeology's ability to satisfy this curiosity will only get better. Every year new techniques come online that push the boundaries of what we can learn from the humble potsherd, stone flake, and bone scrap. You've heard of radiocarbon dating (which can date anything organic as long as it's no more than 45,000 years old), but you are probably not familiar with our many other dating techniques, such as optically stimulated luminescence, which dates the last time that quartz grains were exposed to sunlight, or electron-spin resonance, which dates teeth based on changes in their molecular structure caused by background radiation in the surrounding sediment.

Analysis of carbon, nitrogen, and strontium isotopes in human bone and teeth tell us what people ate and where they were born and raised; these also help trace people's movements across a landscape. We can extract lipids from the walls of ceramic vessels, and identify what foods were cooked or stored in the pot. We can extract protein residue from a stone tool and name the animal killed or butchered. We can identify animal bones to the species level (in fact, that's the easy part), and we can tell if those animals were butchered by humans or gnawed by dogs, wolves, or rodents. We can tell you if a coprolite (desiccated human feces) was left by a man or woman, and what that person ate. We can tell if the human handprints that decorate many caves around the world are those of men or women (it has to do with hand size and digit ratios). We can trace stone tools and the clay or temper used to make pottery back to their geological sources; the same data help us track nomadic movements or trade routes. We can even extract genetic material from ancient skeletal remains. We can learn a lot.

But, to be honest, we can apply many of these techniques only in particular cases, and all have their limitations. I gave you a detailed description of Ötzi to let you in on a trade secret: archaeology cannot *systematically* recover such detailed information. Not all sites preserve DNA or, in fact, any organic material, and there are always potential sources of contamination. Many sites are not places where people lived, but are places, such as stream deltas, where Mother Nature dumped artifacts and bones after eroding them out of their original sites. Although we will continue to push the corners of the envelope and extract more information from even the most humble of archaeological objects, archaeologists will never be able to create as detailed a picture of the past as we would like.

But as my first mentor, David Hurst Thomas, said, it's not what archaeologists find that matters, it's what we find out. Ötzi and his kit are what we found, but what we want to find out is a different matter. The study of Ötzi gives us one man's biography, but how much can that tell us about Neolithic life in southern Europe? Imagining the past as a family photograph, Ötzi stands out clearly, but the rest of his kin are pixilated and smudged. Ötzi alone cannot tell us much about the longer term, large-scale processes of technological, social, political, and cultural life of the Neolithic. But, in fact, archaeology *can* see those processes, and often quite clearly.

. . .

To examine these larger processes, we have to study data that don't give us such a personal connection to the past, or a sense that "we are there." But that's OK, and a British archaeologist with the wonderful name of Osbert Guy Stanhope Crawford (1886–1957) tells us why.

Born in India and orphaned by the age of eight, Crawford studied geography and cartography in school, although his real interest was prehistory. He managed to find his way onto an excavation in the Sudan in 1911, but the First World War interrupted his career.[2]

During the war Crawford worked in the Royal Flying Corps as an observer, taking and interpreting photographs until he was shot down in 1918; he spent the remainder of the war in a German POW camp. After the war, he took a post in Britain's Ordinance Survey, using aerial photography to look for unexploded bombs. In shooting photos from the side of a biplane with the sun low in the sky, Crawford discovered patterns of shadows. He soon learned these were buried walls and ditches, so large and yet so subtle as to escape detection by a pedestrian on the ground. (Crawford demonstrated this point by showing how a carpet's patterns were obvious in a photo taken while he was standing, but obscured in one taken from his cat's point of view.) His approach helped archaeologists discover many ceremonial spaces marked by ditches and embankments in the English countryside.

Crawford wanted to create a forum where the results of archaeologists' work could be shared. In 1927 he created the journal *Antiquity,* which today is a major publication of world archaeology. In the inaugural issue, he explained the journal's subject: "our field is the Earth, our range in time a million years or so, our subject the human race." This statement succinctly describes the twin strengths of archaeology: time and space.

No other science regards humans on archaeology's scale. We "see" human behavior as it is manifested over wide reaches of geography and long reaches of time. Archaeology studies the *whole* range of humanity—from before we were human until today, from the equator to the poles. I admit that we can't see the detail that cultural anthropologists or historians can, and we only rarely see the individuals of the past, people such as Ötzi. We cannot systematically reconstruct religions, cosmology, kin terms, or any of the more abstract aspects of human culture that are often only indirectly manifested in the remains we recover. I can't tell you how many times someone from the public has visited one of my excavations and asked me, "What was their religion like?" I hate to disappoint them. But with so much time and space at our disposal, we make up for the lack of details with the big picture. As I like to tell students, archaeologists may not always see the trees, but we capture the forest with great clarity.

. . .

Archaeologists are interested in ancient people's behaviors and thoughts, but we can get to their behaviors and thoughts only through what they left behind: broken bones, burnt seeds, bits of pottery . . . a collapsed temple if we're lucky. We rely on *things* for our story, and more to the point, we rely on patterns in the occurrence of things over time and space.

New students of prehistory quickly learn the importance of terms like *periods* and *phases,* terms that refer to units of time and space. In the American Southwest, for example, you might hear us talk about the Basketmaker period, or Pueblo I and Pueblo II. These terms refer to periods of time; the Basketmaker period, for example, runs from about 200 B.C. to A.D. 700, Pueblo I from A.D. 700 to 900, and Pueblo II from A.D. 900 to 1100. These terms refer not only to time but also to space, because they're used only in the American Southwest, not elsewhere.

Phases are defined by spatial and temporal distributions of certain kinds of things, such as house styles, arrowhead shapes, or pottery decorations. For example, the Basketmaker period was a time in the American Southwest when people lived in semisubterranean pithouses and made excellent baskets (hence the period's name) and some pottery; we also find modest amounts of the remains of maize, such as burnt corncobs. The Pueblo I phase marks the appearance of the familiar square, above-ground pueblo, as well as kivas (round, semisubterranean religious structures), some black-on-white pottery (black geometric designs on a white background), and some red painted pottery. Maize detritus is common on Pueblo I sites and signals a shift in the importance of maize to the diet. In Pueblo II times, pueblos become larger, and a few massive kivas appear. Modest grayware pottery is now corrugated, and black-on-white pottery becomes abundant. There's much more to it, but these differences in material remains are why Southwestern archaeologists divide space and time in the way that they do.

Here's the important point: archaeologists talk about change in terms of these phases because we assume that a change in material remains signals a change in the organization of human society. In a textbook, we might write a chapter describing "what happened" during Basketmaker times, a description of the people's subsistence and their social and political organization as we interpret it from material remains. Another chapter would use the material remains of Pueblo I sites to relate how subsistence and social and political life changed from Basketmaker times. This is not easy, yet breathing life into material remains is what archaeology is all about—going from the static remains of the past to the dynamic behavior that produced them.

. . .

However, I'm sure that if the people who lived through an archaeological phase were to read our chapter they'd be disappointed. "You didn't talk about the terrible winter when Coyote Woman died with her children," they might say. "And what about Red Hand, that wonderful singer and hunter? You said nothing about him."

Let me describe this shortcoming in a manner that's a little closer to home. Imagine if I asked you to write a five-hundred-word essay on what happened in the twentieth century. What would you include? More important, what would you leave out? World War I? World War II? The Korean conflict? Vietnam? The League of Nations? The United Nations? The 1919 flu epidemic? The Depression? The polio vaccine? The moon landing? Polar expeditions? Computers? Communism? The Internet? Einstein? Curie? Spielberg? AIDS? The double helix? Women's suffrage? The civil rights movement? Gandhi? The Kennedy assassinations? Television? Satellites? The 1973 oil embargo? Martin Luther King? Bob Dylan? Duke Ellington? Elvis? Muhammad Ali? Madonna? Cell phones? Microchips? This is a daunting assignment, but it's much like what archaeologists do. We sort through the details to find the pattern, the forest.

How should you tackle this assignment? By now you might be able to guess: expand your vision. Southwestern archaeologists see patterns in time and space not by myopically focusing on a single site, but by looking at many sites of different ages over thousands of square miles. Doing so allows them to see what made Basketmaker and Pueblo I sites different. So, to write your essay on the twentieth century, you would have to study the eighteenth and nineteenth centuries (and it would help if you had the twenty-first and twenty-second as well). This would help you see what was truly different and special about the twentieth century.

And remember, archaeologists can study only the past's material remains. When we look for patterns in space and time, we look for patterns in the distribution of material remains. But archaeologists are actually not that interested in material things (they're just what we find). Instead, we're interested in what those things have to say about the organization of past human societies (that's what we find out).

Think about excavating trash dumps from the eighteenth, nineteenth, and twentieth centuries: what do you think would stand out? Besides a difference in the sheer volume of stuff, several things might catch your attention in the trash of the twentieth century: vehicles and their accoutrements, electronic appliances, and tons and tons of paper (the late Bill Rathje, an interesting archaeologist who studied modern trash, found that recyclable paper took up the most space in landfills).[3] The archaeologist would use such stark differences in material remains to create two phases, one representing the twentieth century and beyond, and one representing the eighteenth and nineteenth centuries.

That's just the beginning of course, for the archaeologist would want to know what cars, electronics, and paper were all about—how were they manufactured and used? Who used them—men, women, children? Were they made locally, or traded? Did they signal prestige, or were they everyday items? We would turn to archaeology's vast array of techniques to answer such questions.

Now you know something about how archaeologists think: We look for spatial and temporal patterns in the distribution of material remains and then use those material remains to reconstruct past human life. We assume that the appearance of new classes of material items—such as stone tools, pottery, square houses, formal religious structures, cars, electronics, and the printed word—all signal an associated change in how human life was organized.

The following chapters will take archaeology's strength, its ability to see patterns in vast reaches of space and time, to its extreme and look for global patterns over the entire course of human history. Imagine taking a seat up in the stratosphere—think of it as the back row of an IMAX theater—and watching a film that depicts all of human history, all six million years of it. As you munch on your popcorn (you'll need the jumbo size), let your vision embrace the entire history of humanity and ask: Do we see any *global* changes in material culture over time? Do we see any phases that encompass the world, that mark major transitions in human evolution, times when the fundamental character of human life on earth changed?

If we could watch human history unfold from such a perch, I think we would see four major times of change, times that introduce significant shifts in the material signature of human history and in the organization of human life. In chapters 3 through 6, we'll see what archaeologists know about each of these transitions. We haven't figured out the entire story yet, but a century ago we knew almost none of it. And we'll see that, contrary to what the despondent student in chapter 1 thought, the way things are today is not how they were in the past. Finally, in chapter 7, we will see that the approach taken in chapters 3 through 6 allows us also to say that the way things are today is not how they will be in the future.

CHAPTER 3

Sticks and Stones

The Beginning of Technology

The past is never dead; it's not even past.

—William Faulkner, *Requiem for a Nun*

Archaeologists are good at finding coins. That's because when we're working, we usually walk with our heads down, scanning the ground. Such a practice becomes habit, and while it doesn't help us find stone tools in town, we can finish the day with a pocketful of spare change. But that's just a side benefit. Our real purpose is to spot artifacts, humanly manufactured things, against a background of rock and earth, even when those artifacts are nothing more than small, dirty fragments. We can do this while walking at a good clip across a plowed field or a desert hillside.

But even a seasoned archaeologist might have a hard time identifying the earliest stone tools. Just simple flakes detached from a larger stone, or cobbles battered from use, these artifacts often don't look much different from other rocks eroding out of a hillside.

The earliest known stone tools were found in Kenya and are about 3.3 million years old.[1] They're the beginning of technology, a crucial piece of the human adaptive strategy that would eventually result in cities, planes, bridges, cars, lunar rovers, artificial limbs, and computers (as well as iPods and cell phones, but nothing's perfect). Those stone tools also set humans on a path that would lead us to alter our environment dramatically. They mark a time when everything changed.

But I'm getting ahead of myself. To understand the importance of stone tools, we have to go back before 3.3 million years ago. The beginnings described in this book often required a great deal of time; they were not overnight revolutions. And, often, several things had to intersect for a new beginning to take place. It's as if innovations, pressures, adaptations, and capacities build up to a crucial tipping point . . . and then humanity goes through a pervasive change. Many see human history as an inexorable move upward, as a story of progress. But remember that evolution doesn't care about any of us. It doesn't care if we "move up." The changes we discuss are not simply "great leaps forward." There is a story to humanity, but it's not a simple one of a mythical hero surviving tests, conquering evil, and finding true love, as attractive as that is.

So where to start? Winston Churchill once said, "The farther backward you can look, the farther forward you can see." We could start with the Big Bang fourteen billion years ago, but that seems excessive, so let's jump ahead to the beginning of our branch of the evolutionary tree, the primate line.

. . .

The first primates showed up around fifty-five million years ago—about 10 million years after a meteor brought about the dinosaurs' demise. The earliest primates were adapted to tropical forests, and they were arboreal—they lived in trees. Primates proved to be a highly adaptive species, and they diversified and moved into a range of environments. New World monkeys split off from the Old World group sometime between thirty-five and forty million years ago, about the time that plate tectonics ripped South America and Africa apart. (Some suggest they arrived in the New World via accidental voyages across the once-narrow Atlantic Ocean on rafts of vegetation washed out of rivers.) The primates who stayed behind in the Old World eventually gave rise to the apes about twenty-five million years ago. This is where we come in.

The apes today include the gibbon, a so-called lesser ape (they would probably resent the term), and the great apes: orangutans, gorillas, chimpanzees, bonobos,[2] and us. Chimpanzees and bonobos are our closest relatives. Our understanding of human evolution is a moving target, but to the best of our knowledge, the line that would eventually evolve into humans diverged from a common ancestor with chimpanzees and bonobos at the end of the Miocene epoch, about seven million years ago. We know this from two sources: DNA and fossils.

You've perhaps heard that chimpanzees and human share 98 percent of their DNA.[3] The small genetic differences arose largely as a function of mutation, random changes in the genetic code. Such changes provide a clue as to when we humans said good-bye to the other primates and began traveling down our own evolutionary path. We know about when some modern human populations split away from others and geneticists use those estimates to calculate the rate of genetic mutation. Using that rate, they can calculate how much time has passed to create the genetic differences between chimps and humans today. Doing so, they estimate that the line that would become humans split off from the line that would continue on as chimps and bonobos about seven million years ago. It's a ballpark figure, but it's probably fairly accurate.

Scientists who study the skeletal remains of our most ancient ancestors are known as paleoanthropologists. The field began in the mid-nineteenth century, when quarry workmen discovered Neanderthal remains in a German limestone cave, and, later, when the Dutch physician Eugene Dubois, searching for the "missing link," found human fossils in Indonesia. The field really took off, though, after 1924, when the Australian anatomist Raymond Dart freed a fossilized australopithecine ("southern ape") skull from a block of limestone found in a South African quarry. (Lacking the proper tools, he famously chipped it out with his wife's knitting needles; history doesn't record what she thought of this.) In 1959, Louis and Mary Leakey discovered the skull of *Zinjanthropus* in Olduvai Gorge in Tanzania (today the specimen is labeled *Australopithecus boisei* or *Paranthropus boisei;* I've always thought the specimen's nickname of "Zinj" was cooler). Paleoanthropologists have not been at the job for very long, but they've done a remarkable job of reconstructing our family tree (see figure 1).

To create that tree, paleoanthropologists must classify their discoveries—a toe or leg bone or, if they're lucky, a skull—in terms of species. That's what leads to all the long names in figure 1. Paleoanthropological discoveries usually show up as dozens or even hundreds of tiny fragments eroding from a hot desert hillside or scattered about in a cave's cool sediments. They are collected, mapped, cleaned, and painstakingly pieced back together. To decide whether a bone represents a new species, the paleoanthropologist must ask if the specimen is similar or dissimilar to other finds. Of course, it is usually both similar *and* dissimilar to other finds. One skull might contain a mandible that is like that of another known skull, but with a differently shaped cranium. Sometimes, the differences are so great that the paleoanthropologists declare them evidence of a new species. This excites everyone and usually causes fierce debates.

Why? Because species tend to occupy their own niches, and which niches are occupied by whom, and in what way, tells us a lot about the

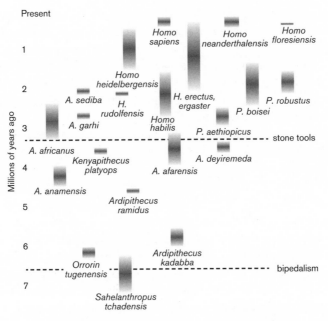

FIGURE 1. The different hominin species of the past seven million years. Although paleoanthropologists agree on the broad outline, many of the specific relationships and species designations are debated. The *A.* stands for the genus *Australopithecus;* the *P.* for *Paranthropus* (which some would classify as *Australopithecus*); the *H.* stands for *Homo,* our own genus.

evolutionary process. Declaring a fossil to represent a new species is a bit of an illusion, because by definition organisms belong to the same species if they breed in the wild and produce fertile offspring. We can't know if two of our ancient ancestors would have "done it" and, if they had, if they would have produced fertile offspring. Instead, paleoanthropologists use standards for determining whether a new set of skeletal remains is similar enough to be categorized with an existing species, or so dissimilar that it can be called a new species. Sometimes the dissimilarities are so great that the remains wind up in an entirely different genus.

Collectively, we refer to all those creatures that are in the human line, including us, as *hominins.* The earliest hominin we know of is *Sahelanthropus tchadensis;* the genus means "ape of the Sahel" (the Sahel is a biogeographic belt that runs just south of the Sahara), and the species name reflects its discovery in Chad. *Sahelanthropus* lived about seven million years ago. This is close to the geneticists' age of divergence, so it comes as no surprise that it shares some skeletal characteristics with chimpanzees (a small brain) and some with later hominins (small canine teeth). And if *Sahelanthropus* is ever voted out of our family history, there is Kenya's *Orrorin tugenensis,* about six million years old, with large canines (an ancient primate trait) but thick tooth enamel (a characteristic shared with later hominins).

One more important thing: the shape of their femurs tells us that both *Sahelanthropus* and *Orrorin* were bipedal; they walked on two legs.

. . .

We think nothing of walking, but bipedalism is actually "risky business," as British anthropologist John Napier once said.[4] Without remarkable and constant fine-tuning of muscle movements, we'd fall with every step, whether or not we were chewing gum. Bipedalism is not just a matter of standing up straight. It requires changes to the lower spine, the pelvis and its muscles, the leg bones (femur and tibia), the foot bones, the knee, and even the skull (the foramen magnum, the hole in the skull's base through which the spinal cord passes, must be centered beneath the skull rather than located toward its back, as it is in chimps).

Chimpanzees can walk on two feet, but they swagger like drunken sailors, and they can't straighten their legs, meaning they must use their muscles, rather than locked knees, to stand upright. They also have to hold their heads up to see straight ahead because of the position of their foramen magnum. For chimps, walking on two feet is a tiring activity.

Nonetheless, a career in trees without the benefit of a prehensile tail (which only New World monkeys have) meant that Old World primates did plenty of branch walking, which preadapted them for bipedalism. With only a few genetic mutations, arboreal apes could be crossing the savanna on two feet (shakily at first, but the adaptation improved with time). But what would push such an evolutionary change?

Hominins appeared at the sunset of the Miocene, a geologic era from about 23 million to 5 million years ago, during which Africa's climate became cooler and drier and extensive grasslands appeared, followed by the evolution of many grazing herd mammals. These created a buffet line for large carnivores, and they, too, became more abundant. As the grasslands expanded, the forest patches that had harbored primates for so long began to shrink. And those shrinking forest patches increased competition among the arboreal primates.

Biological structures predisposing a Miocene ape to bipedalism might have been a problem in the mid-Miocene, but by the late Miocene those arboreal apes with the biological capacity for bipedalism could have moved between patches of forest. This gave them a selective advantage: they could get to food resources that exclusively arboreal primates would find more difficult to procure.[5] (That adaptation could also have been flight, but primates were not preadapted for that, so flying monkeys today are found only in fictional witches' lairs.)

But why not use all four feet to scamper to the next stand of trees? What's so useful about walking on two feet? A lot, actually. A two-legged primate can stand up and reach food (as chimps do) that a four-legged primate would find challenging. A two-legged primate can move more efficiently between patches, since two-legged walking uses less energy than four-legged walking, and a bipedal ape can stand up to survey for danger (as meerkats do), which comes in handy in a savanna filled with carnivores. In addition, by standing upright, a two-legged primate exposes less of its body's surface area directly to the hot African sun and thus requires about two-thirds the water of a similarly sized four-legged primate. And two-legged primates could still go after food in the trees, climbing them just as you and I do.

Note that the bipedal adaptation was selected so that *Sahelanthropus* could keep on being what it was, an arboreal primate. But in trying to be a good arboreal primate, natural selection turned *Sahelanthropus* into something new. Walking bipedally also freed up the hands. This might have made it easier for *Sahelanthropus* to provision offspring, because food could be carried back to camp. Or it might have made it possible to carry those offspring while foraging, meaning that they were not left behind at a nest, vulnerable to predators and accidents.

Hands-free walking also meant the new primates could carry tools. This doesn't mean that bipedalism evolved in order to carry tools; that would be like saying we evolved complex intelligence in order to solve calculus problems. In fact, walking across the savanna, *Sahelanthropus* most likely didn't carry tools.

When I say *tools,* I mean stone tools. Archaeologists can study only the things that have survived what Sir Francis Bacon called "the shipwreck of time," and for the oldest archaeological sites, stone and fossilized bone are all that remain. But you are probably thinking, what about tools fashioned from wood, such as digging sticks? Perhaps the earliest hominins walked across the savanna with a sharpened stick that served as a digging tool and spear. Maybe, but I doubt it, because stone tools are needed to fashion wood into tools, to turn a stick into a sharpened stick. A technology of wood would still result in some stone tools. And stone tools don't appear until long after *Sahelanthropus* and *Orrorin* exit the stage.

. . .

The earliest stone tools are called *Oldowan tools,* named after Olduvai Gorge in Tanzania, where paleoanthropologists first found them in the 1930s. Although humans would eventually develop some clever ways to make stone implements and fashion some beautiful tools, Oldowan tools were not fancy. Still, they were effective, and hominins used them for about two million years.

Making stone tools requires knowledge and skill. For starters, you have to know what kinds of rock can be flaked; these include fine-grained basalt and rhyolite, as well as quartzite and chert (aka "flint" or "jasper"). Oldowan toolmakers apparently understood this. They also appreciated fracture mechanics. Oldowan tools were made using percussion knapping—striking one large rock with another to remove flakes. Strike the right kind of rock with just the right amount of force, at just the right angle, and at just the right place and you'll remove a sharp, useful flake.

The tools also indicate forethought because some had been left in sites, where archaeologists have found them, many kilometers from the rock's point of geologic origin. Sometimes, hominins carried stones as far as twenty kilometers. Clearly, our ancestors were thinking ahead.

And this means that these tool-using hominins were cognitively beyond chimps. Modern chimps use numerous tools, including twigs stripped of their leaves to "fish" for protein-rich termites (Jane Goodall was the first to observe this), stone anvils and "hammers" to break open nuts, and crushed leaves to soak up water in tree hollows. But chimps don't make and use stone tools like those found in Olduvai Gorge. Archaeologists Nick Toth and Kathy Schick taught Kanzi, a bonobo, how to make flake tools and to use those tools to cut the string on a box containing food.[6] But Kanzi never mastered the percussion technique. Instead, she often just threw the core at the ground and then picked up a flake to cut the string. Although chimps in the wild use several kinds of tools, no one has ever seen them fashion stone flakes. And chimps rarely transport objects more than twenty or thirty meters.

. . .

What were the stone tools used for? Because the stone tools are found with the bones of possible game animals, we suspect the two have something to do with one another. In a few cases archaeologists have found stone tool cut marks on the bones, showing that flake tools were used at least some of the time to butcher animals. But did the hominins hunt those animals, or did they scavenge them?

The debate over whether our stone tool–using ancestors were hunters or scavengers was in full swing when I was a graduate student in the early 1980s. In one of my classes the late Frank Livingstone gave rousing support for Louis Leakey's argument that the early hominins were serious hunters, taking down animals many times their own size. I pointed out that the alleged death-delivering tools were hardly more than lumps of rock, that throwing them would only annoy a large animal, and, moreover, that the hominins who allegedly threw them stood only about four feet tall. Livingstone became red in the face and went into one of his characteristic tirades, finishing with "They were really clever; they could roll and dodge with the punches. You just don't want to believe that your ancestors were bloodthirsty killers!" I replied that I didn't care if australopithecines ate their children, I just wanted a valid argument. (I didn't do well in that course.)

Flakes from Oldowan tools are not the sort of thing that could be hafted onto the tip of a spear, but they could be used to whittle a stick into a simple spear. Early hominins could have hunted small game with such a tool. But large game is a different matter. Solid evidence of large-game hunting, in fact, appears only 300,000 years ago—the age of a number of long wooden spears preserved in a bog in Germany, found lying near horse remains.[7]

Seeking to understand the potential of scavenging as a niche, some archaeologists have studied dead animals on the modern savanna, measuring how much meat is left on carcasses. (By the way, most archaeologists classify such research as "awesome.") These studies show that a hominin could do pretty well if it got to a carcass early, before the lions, hyenas, and vultures had their fill, or perhaps if it drove away those predators and scavengers. What's the role of stone tools in this?

To answer that question means understanding that evolution is about trade-offs in the costs and benefits of different biological structures or behaviors. A bipedal primate, for example, will have problems living in trees full-time, but it can trade efficient life in the trees for the benefit of moving between patches of forest. The benefit of the mutations that permitted bipedalism did not outweigh their costs until forests shrank in the arid late Miocene environment and increased selective pressures on arboreal primates. Likewise, there were costs and benefits to stone tools. Stone tools had a cost in their manufacture, in learning how to make them, and in transporting the cobbles from their geologic origin to where they were needed. What was their benefit?

Imagine finding a carcass of a large animal; the carnivores have left, or you've driven them off. A carnivore such as a lion will leave some meat on a carcass because it can't get to it all with only its mouth. It takes the best and leaves the rest (for vultures and bone-eating hyenas). If you had some way to remove the last bits, you could walk off with a decent haul of food. And if you could break open the leg bones, you could retrieve the marrow, which pound for pound contains more than twice the calories of meat.

Acquiring food efficiently is job one for any organism; if a species fails at that task, it's doomed. As competition for food increases, organisms tend to specialize; if they're good at their specialty, they push other organisms out. The losers must find sustenance among foods that might be harder to find, procure, and process. Natural selection can produce organisms with specialized biological adaptations to obtain particular kinds of food. Darwin's many kinds of Galapagos finches, for example, had beaks that were each selected to feed on particular seeds or insects, specific parts of cacti, or insects in particular locations (e.g., in the crevices of tree bark).

Natural selection might have eventually produced a primate with jaws capable of the vice-like crushing force needed to break open the bones of large game and procure the marrow, or with a mouth and teeth that could scrape meat off a carcass. That's not only a scary thought, but it's highly unlikely, given the many changes that would be required in primate skull form, musculature, and tooth shape.

On the other hand, an organism that develops technology can leap-frog the long process of biological selection and cut to the front of the evolutionary queue. So the costs and benefits of stone tools tell us that hominins upped their game in the late Miocene competitive environment and that they probably did so from close to the bottom of the evolutionary scrum pile. Technology allowed them to win harder-to-acquire foods at an energetic gain. They might have started as scavengers (we don't actually know), but they eventually used stone tools to hunt animals.

Another food source might have lain below ground: roots, bulbs, corms, and tubers. Capuchin monkeys dig up shallow roots with stones,[8] and hominins could have hit on the idea of sharpening a digging stick with a stone tool and using it to get at deeper tubers, down 50 or 75 centimeters.

With stone tools, those small, two-legged hominins that had been living by trekking from forest patch to forest patch moved into a new niche. With their hands free, they were preadapted for stone tool use: to carry cobbles to where they might be needed, to cut or scrape meat from large carcasses, to make digging sticks to dig up tubers, or to fashion simple spears to hunt small game. Technology opened up a new niche for two-legged hominins.

Who were these tool-using hominins? Unfortunately, no one left any "fingerprints" on the tools. If you look back at figure 1, you'll see that at 3.3 million years ago the toolmakers were probably one of the australopithecines.[9] No doubt we'll debate the question until we find a hominin clutching a stone flake in its skeletal hand (and yes, that's highly unlikely). No matter—tools gave some hominins an advantage. They extracted more energy from their environment and outcompeted their non-tool-using hominin neighbors. And for their trouble, they evolved into our genus, *Homo*, a fully fledged tool-using hunter.

Technology was a game changer, the first tipping point, the first beginning for a new kind of primate.

. . .

We're fairly certain that by the time the *Homo* line rose, about two million or more years ago, our ancestors were eating a broad diet that probably included meat. How do we know that? A hominin that eats seeds, roots, and tubers has teeth with telltale pits and striations. But the teeth of some australopithecines and of *Homo*, especially *Homo erectus*, are not so pitted and etched, so they were probably eating a more generalized diet. The teeth of *Homo erectus* are also smaller but with rougher chewing surfaces perhaps created through natural selection to shear through meat. A diet of mostly seeds is associated with large, flat-surfaced teeth selected for grinding.[10]

Moreover, the body of *Homo*, already adapted for bipedalism, may have also been adapted for hunting. In 1984, Kenyan paleoanthropologist Kamoya Kimeu made the remarkable discovery of a nearly complete *Homo erectus* skeleton, that of a young boy. That child, known as Nariokotome boy (named after a spot near Kenya's Lake Turkana) was about eight years old when he died, and he had a modern pelvis and relatively long arms and legs.[11] (This boy's life history was more chimp-like than human-like, and he attained adult size at an earlier age than do modern humans.) We don't know everything that Nariokotome could do, but his leg bones tell us that he could run. What does that have to do with hunting?

After carnivores such as cheetahs, lions, and leopards sight their prey, they stalk it, getting as close as possible before exploding into a chase. But they will chase the game for only a short time. They expend a lot of energy in running, and if they can't snag their prey quickly, they cut their losses and give up.

Humans are different. As a bipedal organism, we are designed to be mobile, not just for quick spurts but also for long distances; this is why humans can become ultrarunners. Prey animals adapt to the behavior of their predators. If an antelope can outrun a lion for just a short while, it knows it will be safe. But that doesn't work when the hunter is a hominin. Modern hunter-gatherers sometimes practice "endurance hunting," during which they literally run an animal to death. By relentless pursuit—sometimes running, sometimes just trotting or walking—they keep an animal moving until it becomes exhausted and easier to kill. Once poisons and effective projectile technology came into use (long after the first stone tools), hunters could practice this form of hunting even more easily, with the poison or bleeding induced by a stone-tipped projectile slowing the animal further. Evolution works with the attributes you already have. If a carnivorous niche was a good one to occupy on the savanna (and it is unless you're preadapted to eating large volumes of grass), then we could expect natural selection to produce a bipedal, primate hunter who could run and carry stone tools.

. . .

Fire might also have been an important element of this new technological adaptation. Fire provides warmth and light at night as well as protection from predators; it also allows a hominin to cook dinner. Cooking increases the value of meat by breaking it down and doing some of the digestive tract's work in advance; it also makes meat much easier to chew.[12] Cooking also converts carbohydrates in tubers into more easily digestible sugars. A hominin eating cooked food can get away with smaller guts because cooking does some of the digestion for it.

Obviously, guts don't preserve, but we can reconstruct them from the skeleton, because primates with large guts have a bell-shaped rib cage; those with smaller guts (like us) have a straighter one. Primates with large guts eat lots of greens; since greens have low food value, the primate must eat a lot. The fearsome gorilla, for example, eats about forty pounds of leaves each day. *Paranthropus* and *Australopithecus* have more bell-shaped rib cages; *Homo* has a straighter one. This suggests that *Homo* ate a more efficient diet, one that we've already seen probably included meat, and perhaps barbeque, because cooked meat, it turns out, is brain food.

Cooked meat, even if it makes up only 10 to 20 percent of the diet, can have a perceptible effect on energetic efficiency. Hominins who cooked their food could spend less time foraging, and more of the energy they acquired could go toward some organ more interesting (and useful to natural selection) than the large intestine. And that more interesting organ was apparently the brain.

Your brain is an expensive organ; it makes up 2.5 percent of your body weight, but requires 20 percent of your energy. By cooking food, *Homo* diverted energy that had been spent on maintaining a massive gut to maintaining a large brain.[13] This may be what helped drive another hallmark of humans, a brain that is large relative to our body size. Early *Homo* had a brain that was 30 percent larger than that of *Australopithecus,* and later *Homo* had a brain 20 percent larger than that of early *Homo.* Cooking made it possible to get more out of meat and tubers, and stone tools increased the ease with which tubers and hunted or scavenged meat were acquired.

If early *Homo* ate cooked meat, then they used fire. Do we have any evidence for that? You might think an ancient hearth would be easy to find, but it's not. Hunter-gatherers don't often build a fire as Boy Scouts do, with an easy-to-spot rock ring. Cutting wood is hard work, especially with a stone axe, and if a log is too big to break over one's knee, foragers simply throw it on the fire. A rock ring would just get in the way of a large log, so foragers don't bother with them. In fact, they usually bring the ends of three long logs together in the hearth's center; as the logs burn, the foragers simply pull the ends together to keep the fire going. (In Madagascar I learned to do this with care. We slept by our hearth, and I would reach out of my sleeping bag before dawn to stoke the fire by pulling the ends of the logs together. The first cold morning I did this, I was startled by two dusty puppies that leapt up yipping; sometime in the night they had hunkered down in the hearth's warm ash.) Surviving evidence of such hearths (fire-reddened earth, charcoal, and ash) can be destroyed by burrowing rodents, earthworms, and soil geochemistry.

So it's understandable that the physical evidence of fire is meager. Archaeologists have located hearths at a site in Israel that are nearly

800,000 years old; another in a South African cave appears to be a million years old. Most evidence for fire, however, appears after 400,000 years ago.[14] Fire was at first most likely "captured" from lightning strikes and kept by moving a few live coals from camp to camp (remember that Ötzi was probably carrying such coals in a bark container lined with green leaves). We'll keep on looking, but right now direct evidence for fire early in our history is limited.

. . .

Technology was part of an adaptive complex that entailed bipedalism, changes in diet, and eventually the use of fire. Technology was especially important because it became a crucial part of the human adaptation. Nothing that followed in human history would have been possible without our ability to use *things* to fulfill our needs; in fact, those humble Oldowan tools were the beginning of space travel. And technology is a crucial part of social interactions, for example, as trade goods, status symbols, and weaponry.

Equipped with even a simple technology, *Homo* extracted more energy from the environment than their competitors. As a result, the *Homo* population eventually replaced the other hominins. The "gracile" Australopithecines disappeared about 1.8 million years ago. Their more robust cousins, *Paranthropus boisei* and *robustus*, hung on a little longer, but they too exited the stage by 1.2 million years ago. Technology must have played a crucial role here because eventually the last hominins left standing on the African savanna, our genus, *Homo*, had stone tools in their hands.

The *Homo* population grew and moved into new lands.[15] Some slipped across the Arabian Peninsula and on to neighborhoods in southern Asia. Paleoanthropologists have found their remains in Indonesia (1.6–1.8 million years old), in the Republic of Georgia (1.8 million years old), and in China (750,000 years).[16] About 800,000 years ago, an African population moved through the Sahara (which contained lakes at the time) and across the Strait of Gibraltar into southern Europe; others entered Europe via the Arabian Peninsula and Turkey. We call those hominins in Europe *Homo heidelbergensis,* and they probably gave rise to *Homo neanderthalensis*—the much-maligned Neanderthals (more on them in the next chapter).

Stone tool technology changed very little between 3.3 and 1.5 million years ago—that's almost two million years of the same damn tools. They were eventually replaced by what archaeologists call *Acheulian* technology. Named after the site of Saint Acheul in France, where it was first discovered in 1859, Acheulian technology consists of several tool types, including the "hand axe." Hand axes come in different varieties, but they are often large oval- to teardrop-shaped, bifacially (two-sided) flaked tools. We suspect they were general-purpose tools—like a Swiss Army knife, if such a knife had only one blade for all purposes. Acheulian technology would eventually appear over much of Africa, Europe, and southern Asia. It too remained much the same for another million years.

Homo might have won the evolutionary game against other hominin species. But in winning, *Homo* groups raised the competitive stakes among themselves. And the prize was to become something totally new.

. . .

Coupled with bipedalism and fire, tools made hominins more successful than their niche's competitors. Those using tools raised more offspring to adulthood than those who did not, and passed on the genetic material (e.g., for mental structures and fine motor control) that permitted toolmaking and using. That was good news, but change creates new problems just as it solves old ones. Relying on stone tools, for example, added a new task to the hominin's day: finding the appropriate rock and learning how to work it. Our busy workdays began in the lower Paleolithic.

And bipedalism created an even greater problem.

Bipedalism is made possible in part by a change in the structure of the pelvis. For female hominins, this meant a reduction in the length of the birth canal, and that meant that bipedal female hominins who continued to gestate fetuses for a long time had to birth infants who were large relative to the birth canal. Those hominins probably died in childbirth, and only those infants who were, in effect, born prematurely survived and passed on their genetic material.[17]

Being born early means that the offspring of bipedal hominins were essentially helpless. Someone would have to carry a *Homo* infant, and the infant was also probably breast-fed for quite a long time. Modern foragers breast-feed children for upwards of four years. This isn't simply because they think it's a good idea, but because weaning foods are hard to come by in a diet of meat, tubers, and seeds. Children chew hard foods with difficulty until they have their first molars, and those don't descend until a child is five and a half to six and a half years old. Consequently, a hunter-gatherer child who did not breast-feed for four to five years was a child that would not survive.

Breast-feeding means that young children must remain with a woman who is lactating, most likely (but not necessarily) their mother. Since small children can't walk as fast as an adult, they often ride on their mother's shoulders or back. One child is enough of a burden; two might work a mother to death. In fact, Bushman women of southern Africa say that a woman "who has children one after another like an animal has a permanent backache."[18] This fact might have produced an important level of cooperation in hominin society.

After I wrote a book about modern hunter-gatherers, a colleague asked me if there was anything about them that I thought could be extrapolated back in time. Very few things, I replied, but one was the division of labor. Among living hunter-gatherers, men hunt large game, and women collect plant food, small game, and shellfish. There are cases of female hunters (the most well-known is that of Agta women in the Philippines), and these accounts tell us that hunting has little to do with strength and more to do with knowledge (of tracks, signs, and animal behavior), patience, and stealth, none of which is the exclusive property of men. So why don't women in modern foraging societies hunt regularly?

The reason is that they often have breast-feeding children with them, and small children are not compatible with hunting. When I asked Mikea men in Madagascar if I could follow them while they hunted, they often said no. They once explained (politely, to my Malagasy colleagues) that "the *vazaha* [foreigner] will get tired and want to go back to camp; he'll get hungry; he won't be able to keep up; he'll make too much noise." In other words, they thought I would act like a child. And that's a problem because once prey is sighted, *it* dictates what happens. If it moves, then the hunter moves. If it runs across open sand dunes, then the hunter must stealthily follow or move quickly through nearby cover to intercept the animal. And you can't do such things with a small child in tow. In fact, boys in modern hunter-gatherer societies often don't accompany hunters until they are ten to twelve years old.

On the other hand, gathering seeds, berries, or tubers; snagging lizards from beneath rocks; or collecting shellfish can be done with small children. In fact, even very young children can be quite good at foraging for stationary food sources. Many small Mikea children dig tubers, African Hadza children pick berries, and Australian Aboriginal children are adept at catching goannas and gathering shellfish.

But meat is the most desired food. Although they might stuff themselves with tubers and berries, without meat, hunter-gatherers might still claim to be starving. Early hominins probably also sought any opportunity to acquire meat. But if women cannot hunt because they have breast-feeding children in tow, how do they get meat?

Some paleoanthropologists argue that the solution lies in pair-bonding (some might go so far as to call it "marriage," but I would not as that implies a whole set of cultural meanings, and if you peek at the next chapter, you'll see that I don't think hominins at this point in evolution were cultural). Those who argue this position point out that one effect of pair-bonding in many species is a reduction in sexual dimorphism, that is, a reduction in the difference between male and female body size: males no longer battle over females, so it's not just the big, brawny guys who get to mate and pass on their genes. And early *Homo* is not, in fact, particularly sexually dimorphic.

Reconstructing social organization for this very early time in human evolution is beyond our scientific capacity. However, the effects of bipedalism on birth and the need to breast-feed hominin offspring in a foraging environment, coupled with tool-assisted hunting, lead me to conclude that male and female hominins must have developed some form of cooperation that probably included food sharing, possibly between pair-bonded males and females but almost certainly within a hominin troop as a whole. Males may have supplied meat, or women may have assisted one another, for example, by breast-feeding offspring while one mother went hunting.

But I'm getting ahead of the story (in the next chapter we'll see that sharing is actually a very complex behavior). The important point is that from our perch in space we see our ancestors change from arboreal, fruit- and leaf-eating, non-toolmaking primates into something completely different by about 1.5 million years ago: bipedal, ground-dwelling, tool-using, most likely hunting, probably cooking, perhaps pair-bonded hominins. In trying to shape the best arboreal primate possible, evolution turned us into something completely different. The way things were for hominins during the Miocene is not the way things would ever be again.

CHAPTER 4

Beads and Stories

The Beginning of Culture

The past is a foreign country: they do things differently there.
—L. P. Hartley, *The Go-Between*

When my son Matt was young, he would help me work our vegetable garden in Kentucky. I was yanking up weeds one day while he knelt next to me, playing with a toy truck. As one particular weed fell on the pile, he jerked his head up. "A swan!" he exclaimed. I looked around, expecting to see an errant waterfowl in our backyard. But there was only Matt, picking up the weed and saying again, "A swan." It was then that I saw the graceful curve of the bird's neck. People see the world differently: some see swans where others see weeds.

It's our capacity for culture, to see the world differently, that sets humans apart from the other primates. Anthropologists debate when humans acquired this capacity, but sitting on your perch in space, watching the hominin world go by, you can't help but notice something happening between 200,000 and 50,000 years ago. At some point, hominins became cultural beings, *humans* as we know them. This is when we became capable of religious thought; when we could tell stories and use metaphors and analogies; when we could create science, art, music, and poetry; when we could become emotional over a speech or a song.

Both genetic and skeletal data point to Africa as the place where modern humans originated. In fact, we can trace what paleoanthropologists call "archaic" *Homo sapiens* back to about 400,000 years ago there.[1] Biologically modern humans appear in Africa about 200,000 years ago. Genetic data show that these modern humans eventually migrated from Africa and spread throughout Europe and Asia. There they interbred, at least occasionally, with the hominin populations already residing there (e.g., Neanderthals) and eventually completely replaced them. Those who say that we are one family are not just making a hopeful metaphor: humanity is genetically one. And besides being a wonderful counter to racism, this fact also tells us that cultural hominins, modern humans, were incredibly evolutionarily successful. It was the capacity for culture that made us so.

Some anthropologists extend the capacity for culture back to archaic *Homo sapiens*, or even to the beginning of the *Homo* lineage, but I think it arose much more recently. This capacity seems not to be one single thing but rather the combined result of several mental capabilities. I think of the era of human evolution between 1 million and 200,000 years ago as something like putting together a symphony orchestra, with different instruments coming on stage at different times and not all tuned to the same key. But archaeological evidence suggests that sometime after 200,000 years ago, the orchestra is seated, their instruments tuned, ready to play Beethoven's Fifth Symphony.

. . .

Many people think of "culture" as knowledge of opera, fine wine, and Shakespeare. They might think that someone who listens to Bach and reads French novels has more culture than someone who listens to Justin Bieber and watches reality TV. But to anthropologists, no person—and no society—has more or less culture than another. This isn't political correctness; it's recognition of the fact that all human populations have the same *capacity* for culture, that *culture* refers to all human creative activity.

Any anthropologist will also tell you the ability to use symbols is essential to human culture. Symbols are something visual, auditory, or tactile that stands for something with which the symbol has no necessary link. For example, a red circle with a red line running diagonally across it tells us that whatever is in the circle is prohibited; when it contains a cigarette, for example, it means no smoking. But if you were raised in a culture that did not use this symbol, you might make the opposite interpretation: smoking is permitted here.

Or consider a simple wink. In American culture it can mean flirting or a playful conspiracy between two people against a third. But in another culture it might only mean that someone has a bit of dust in their eye. We use symbols all the time; consider what we think clothing, houses, and cars say about their owners.

Symbols matter because the capacity for culture means that humans
understand the world as a symbolic construction. Let me explain what I
mean with an example, one portrayed in the 1983 documentary *First
Contact.* The film is about three white Australian brothers, Daniel,
James, and Michael Leahy, who ventured into the interior of New
Guinea in the 1930s to look for gold. They were the first white people to
set foot in New Guinea's highlands, where they encountered a population of over one million. Neither the New Guineans nor the Australians
knew of the existence of the other, and both had to figure out who the
other was. The film is remarkable not only because we have photos and
footage of the initial encounter between two cultures—remarkably the
Leahy brothers brought along both a still and a movie camera—but also
because the film's makers interviewed the two surviving Leahy brothers
as well as members of the New Guinea population who were youths at
the time of contact. What did each think the other was all about?

Since the Australians were looking for gold, they set about digging
up and sluicing the streambed outside one village. When the village men
eagerly helped them, the Australians interpreted this in the only way
their culture allowed: the New Guinea men were mates looking for a
job to earn a bit of money (in this case, shells). Is that what the New
Guineans thought they were doing?

Many New Guinean peoples practice a form of religion that anthropologists call *ancestor worship.* In it, your deceased ancestors play a
role in the world, and you must maintain a respectful relationship with
them in order to have a successful life. These particular New Guinean
folks often ritually disposed of the cremated bones of the dead in rivers.
The New Guineans decided the Australians were ghosts of the ancestors, who were digging in the river to find their bones. Better help
them out!

Each party interpreted the other's behavior in the only way they
could. And both were wrong because their symbolic constructions of
the world were different. For the capitalist Australians, money and
employer-employee relations drove the world; for the ancestor-worship-
ping New Guineans, one's dead relatives were in the driver's seat. We
say these are different symbolic constructions because each group, the
New Guineans and the Australians, used their culture to interpret
actions (just as we interpret symbols) in a way that makes sense (but
this doesn't mean it's the correct interpretation).

Culture implies an ability to understand the world by interpreting
experience through the lens of an internally consistent, organized body

of thought. This is why sunsets and sunrises, the moon, waves, trees, birds, rocks, mountains, rivers, men, women, children, clothing, food, buildings, songs, flags, and in fact *everything* takes on meaning to humans—though not necessarily the same meanings.

. . .

We assume that the capacity for culture is rooted in biology, specifically in some aspect of the brain's neurology. British archaeologist Steven Mithen has perhaps come close to describing what that biology does.[2] Mithen argues that the mind works with two kinds of intelligence. One of these is general intelligence. Its capacity is reflected in the size of the brain, or, more specifically, the size of the neocortex (the larger outer portion of the brain), which governs the size of our working memory. Greater working memory permits an organism to hold more than one thought in mind and to "put two and two together."

The other kind of intelligence, Mithen argues, is more specific and is contained in four "modules" that store and work with particular kinds of information: (1) a social module that helps us understand the behavior of others; (2) a physics module that helps us understand motion, action, and reaction, that is, the properties of technology; (3) a linguistics module that permits us to speak with a range of sounds and about a range of abstract subjects; and (4) a natural history module that catalogues the behaviors and attributes of plants, animals, and inanimate objects. Mithen argues that chimps have all these modules except the linguistic module.

Humans' "great leap forward," according to Mithen, was *cognitive fluidity*, the neurological linking of these different modules. The human brain comprises some 86 billion neurons, each with an average of 7,000 synaptic connections to other neurons. For comparison, chimps have about 7 billion neurons. Even the elephant, with a larger brain, has only 23 billion. Information storage and connectivity is what the human brain is all about.

With neurological connections between the different modules, we can think about social relationships using thoughts from our natural history module; or we can think about the natural world as technology, objects that can be manipulated to achieve a goal. The linguistic module allows us to talk about these things using knowledge and concepts from the different modules. This means we can use analogies and metaphors. Linking the natural history, social, and linguistic modules together permits us to say "Sam is crafty as a fox." Such a statement makes sense to members of a culture that regards foxes as crafty. The statement might seem odd to members of culture that did not regard foxes as crafty, but it would make no sense whatsoever to someone who cannot understand a metaphor.

This biological capacity to link different realms of knowledge is what permits New Guinea people to look at white people for the first time and see their ancestral spirits come to reclaim their bones. It is the capacity that makes us cultural.

Some anthropologists and many primatologists say that chimpanzees and bonobos have culture, too. They make this claim because behaviors, such as how chimps build their nightly tree nests, vary among chimp troops, are socially learned, and don't reflect functional or environment differences. Some chimps start building nests one way, for whatever reason, and that way is passed down.

But while culture is socially learned, there is more to it, because humans' socially learned behavior produces a worldview, a way of understanding that relies on a symbolic interpretation of the world made possible by cognitive fluidity. Some chimps can indeed learn behaviors that appear to involve the use of symbols, but that might actually be *indexical learning,* in which some act or object is indexed to a desirable outcome, such as food. Chimps cannot, as anthropologist Leslie White was fond of pointing out, appreciate the difference between holy water and distilled water because there is no material difference, only a symbolic one. In this all-important sense, chimps are not cultural.

Given that the capacity for a symbolic construction of the world is central to a definition of humans as cultural, when did this capacity appear? To answer that question, let's first consider another mental capacity, the ability to recognize that others have thoughts. This is a little like mind reading and it's necessary to the capacity for culture because it allows you to know whether you and another person do or do not think in the same way.

. . .

You might have heard of the old vaudeville routine that entails one performer saying to another, "You know that I know that you know that I know . . ." until the audience can no longer keep up and breaks down laughing. This gambit reflects an important element of cognition known as *levels of intentionality.* As I described above, culture entails ideas about how the world operates and about how people should behave.

But culture works only if two members know that each holds the other's beliefs. There are, as the vaudeville sketch implies, an infinite number of levels of intentionality:

1. I know . . .
2. I know that you think . . .
3. I know that you think that we know . . .
4. I know that you think that we know that she thinks . . .
5. I know that you think that we know that she thinks that we know . . .

Realistically, our working memory cannot keep track of more than five levels (and mine conks out at about three). Most animals can reach only one level—they know what they intend and for all they know so does everyone else (or they don't know that knowing what another knows is something they don't know). Chimps reach two levels, possibly three, although that's still not clear.[3] These levels of intentionality are essential to the storytelling that is crucial to passing on culture, especially where the story is one of deception and intrigue (which is the best kind, isn't it?).

At least two levels of intentionality are necessary for an organism to have a *theory of mind*. Theory of mind entails the capacity to know that others have other thoughts, possibly different from your own. Being able to "read minds" is obviously an advantage to a social organism. Having three levels of intentionality is a precursor to culture (I know that you know that we both understand that the ancestors are seeking their bones).

How many levels of intentionality did our hominin ancestors have?

Using studies into the brains and psychology of living humans and primates and measurements on paleontological skull specimens, Robin Dunbar estimated the number of levels of intentionality from the estimated size of grey matter in the frontal lobe of different hominins.[4] It turns out that archaic *Homo sapiens* (of about 100,000 years ago) and Neanderthals come in at four. *Homo erectus* is a little further back with three, and *Homo habilis* and the australopithecines are at two. If correct, then *Homo erectus* could have had the capacity for culture.

But I doubt that *Homo erectus* was the first cultural hominin because a second capacity that is needed to be cultural is language. Without speech, it's hard to pass on abstract ideas such as "the hills were created when animals were human, and when warthog and wildebeest fought over the moon." Language is a precondition for culture, so we need to know when hominins began talking.

. . .

There are about seven thousand different languages spoken in the world today, and in the past there were many more. Each has its own rules for putting sounds together into words, and words together into sentences. Each language gives humans the capacity to talk about complex matters, new experiences, things that don't exist (which means we can lie, but also that we can write science fiction and fantasy), and things that might exist (such as the afterlife, spiritual beings, and gods).

The capacity to learn language is biological. Children in all cultures learn language through similar stages of acquisition without explicit instruction, and if they are deprived of the opportunity before the age of about twelve, they might never learn language very well. (By the way, all children can easily learn a second language before the age of twelve; we should begin foreign language instruction early in grammar school and not wait until high school or, worse, college.) Even people of below-normal intelligence are at least minimally competent speakers of a language. Clearly, the human mind is designed to learn language. When did this capacity arise?

That's a difficult question to answer since words don't fossilize, and written language, such as Egyptian hieroglyphics and cuneiform writing (two of the earliest), appeared only about five thousand years ago. But language entails the biological architecture to produce sounds physically and to produce language mentally. Can we see evidence of these pieces of biology?

Humans physically produce a wide array of sounds because of the position of our larynx. Bipedalism played a role in this. The skull of a two-legged organism sits on top of its spinal cord, and as a result the vertebral column moves closer to the mouth, and the larynx's position shifts, creating a larger chamber in the throat, allowing humans to make a wider array of sounds than, say, chimpanzees. This suggests that we could have had the biological apparatus for language soon after we were bipedal. But this means only that we could make a range of sounds, not necessarily that we were using language as we do today.

Maybe growth in brain size tells us something. Human brain size has steadily increased over time, from early *Homo*'s 650 cubic centimeters (cc) to Nariokotome's 900 cc to our own 1,350 cc. Growth in brain size really took off 500,000 years ago. Was this when language kicked in?

Much of the increase in brain size took place in the neocortex, especially the gray matter of the frontal lobe. The frontal lobe houses our working memory that helps perform the so-called executive functions, such as innovation in problem solving, analogical reasoning, and long-range planning, as well as some linguistic tasks. However, the size of the neocortex also correlates with the intensity of social behavior (e.g., grooming, play, aggressive and sexual displays), so an increase in its size might reflect the increased processing of social information and not necessarily growing linguistic competence. Is there a more direct indicator of language than overall brain size?

Language production and comprehension takes place in several areas of the brain, especially the frontal lobe's inferior frontal gyrus, or IFG (Broca's area, which might be familiar to you, is a portion of the left side of the IFG). The IFG is important not only to language production and comprehension but also to object manipulation, searching, math, and music.

The IFG is also associated with stone tool manufacture.[5] Cognitive scientists use some sophisticated equipment to measure where activity occurs in the brain when a subject is speaking, listening, or doing some activity, such as making stone tools. When modern subjects replicate Oldowan tools, some areas of the IFG (and other portions of the brain) light up, but when replicating an Acheulian hand ax, these areas and others, notably the pars triangularis of the IFG, register activity. Oldowan flake tools don't require much forethought, but making an Acheulian hand ax is a more language-like activity because the flint-knapper must think ahead, imagining how removing one flake will affect future flake removals so that he or she can arrive at the final teardrop-shape form. Language requires its speaker to do the same thing, using words and grammar that depend in part on what comes later in a sentence.

These experiments suggest that language and tool manufacture might have coevolved. If so, then language might appear with Acheulian technology, some 1.7 million years ago. Another possibility, though, is that the brain's architecture was initially selected for stone tool manufacture. Then, later, that architecture was co-opted for language.

When might that have happened? Some archaeologists point not to stone tools themselves, but to multicomponent tools, such as a stone point mounted on a wooden spear, as evidence of a mental architecture that supported both complex technology and language. Archaeologist Lawrence Barham argues that even simple hafted tools require sophisticated thought.[6] For example, a stone point held tightly to a wooden shaft requires (1) acquiring the right kind of stone and knapping it to a size and shape appropriate for the spear's anticipated wooden shaft; (2) fashioning that shaft of the right sort of wood and to the right length, weight, and balance; (3) acquiring the binding, such as leather thongs or sinew fashioned from the ligaments and tendons of animals; and (4) making adhesive, fashioned from a mixture of tree resin and minerals, heated and applied at just the right temperature. Such a technology requires thinking ahead and the ability to mentally put disparate items together into a coherent, sequenced plan of action. That process is structurally similar to language, putting appropriate words into appropriate syntax to form sentences. The earliest evidence we have for multicomponent tools is sometime after 500,000 years ago.

Genetics also provides a clue as to when the biological capacity for language first appeared. The FOXP2 gene is essential to the normal development of language. Geneticists identified this gene in a modern family whose members had disruptions in their facial muscles that created problems in sound production, sound discrimination, and grammar. Although members of this family had normal-sized brains, they had, among several changes, reduced portions of the frontal lobe. Genetic studies show that Neanderthals had the FOXP2 gene, so it probably appeared in the *Homo* line before 800,000 years ago (when the line that would become the Neanderthals split off from the rest of the *Homo* line in Africa and moved to Europe).

Different indicators provide different estimates of when our ancestors started talking, but even if we could determine when language appeared, would that necessarily point to the capacity for symbolic thought? Language consists of symbols: there is no reason that *dog* means "dog" any more than do *chien, koira,* or *alika* (French, Finnish, and Malagasy). But we must be careful not to confuse indexical learning with the use of symbols, and that's easy to do when an organism is capable of sophisticated learning.

For example, several primatologists have tried to teach language to chimps. Since chimps don't have the biological apparatus for speech, trainers use a modified form of American Sign Language. Years ago I met the first chimp taught this sign language; her name was Washoe, and she had learned about 350 signs. Before I entered the facility, the steward taught me a simple greeting. I don't know what I was expecting, but I was shocked when Washoe signed back. Interspecies communication! I hoped she had said something profound, maybe: "Don't worry; everything will be all right." But no. The steward looked a little embarrassed and translated: "Washoe likes your shoes." (Years later, in Washoe's obituary, I learned she was fascinated with everyone's footwear; it was not simply my black Nocona boots that impressed her.)

Chimp language studies reveal that much goes on in the simian mind. Chimps can indeed learn to use hundreds of signs, and some argue that these studies prove chimps have the cognitive capacity for language because they display productivity (by making new words) and displacement (talking about things not at hand). Perhaps, or their capacity might be only complex indexical thinking. The jury is still out.

Language is a crucial component of human culture; without it we could not transmit the complex, abstract information that makes up cultural knowledge. But intense verbal communication is not a direct indicator of culture. By at least 200,000 years ago hominins were most likely communicating with something like language. But when we could talk and when we could talk about cultural matters are possibly two different things.

This means that we must look for evidence of specific behaviors rather than capacities, behaviors that more directly reflect the presence of culture. One of those behaviors might be food sharing.

. . .

During anthropological fieldwork among the Mistassini Cree in the Canadian forests during the 1950s, Eleanor Leacock went on a hunting excursion with a Cree man, Thomas. After several days, they encountered two other hunters who were hungry and who asked for something to eat. Thomas gave away the last of his flour and lard to them, which meant he had to return to camp sooner, with fewer furs than he had hoped to obtain. Leacock asked how he felt about this and whether he expected some payback. She was taken aback by Thomas's response, and she wrote in her journal: "This was one of the very rare times Thomas lost patience with me, and he said with deep, if suppressed anger, 'suppose now, not give them flour, lard—just dead inside.' More revealing than the incident itself were the finality of his tone and the inference of my utter inhumanity in raising questions about his action."[7]

Incidents such as this lead anthropologists to consider sharing an essential part of the foraging lifeway. And, although hunter-gatherers share many things, their attention focuses on the sharing of meat. We've evolved a taste for fatty meat because it's high in calories and nutrients.

If you forget about heart disease, fatty meat is a great choice. So when someone brings a deer or antelope into a hunter-gatherer camp, everyone pays attention and expects a share.

It would be nice if hunters always shared meat out of the goodness of their hearts, but the sharing of meat is often preceded by demands that it be shared. Among southern Africa's Ju/'hoansi, anthropologist and demographer Nancy Howell found that it was "not altruism or saintliness that reinforced sharing . . . but an unending chorus of *na, na, na* ('gimme, gimme, gimme')."[8] Hunters give in to these demands to avoid social sanctions.

Living hunter-gatherers share meat according to cultural rules. Among the Australian Gunwinggu, for example, the head and one of the forequarters of kangaroos and wallabies go to the hunter; the other forequarter goes to the hunter's companion or brother. The rump and tail go to the hunter's mother's brother's son or his mother's brother's daughter's son (in this culture you keep track of these relationships). Each hindquarter goes to a senior man, while the heart, liver, tripe, and other internal organs go to the hunter and senior men, or to other men present at the kill.[9]

Chimps also share meat, but differently. Chimps hunt small animals, especially red colobus monkeys. They do so in a fashion that appears communal—some chimps climb up and chase a monkey through the treetops while others position themselves on the ground, presumably waiting for it to fall; still others climb trees ahead of the hunt, presumably cutting off escape routes. The chimp that makes the kill will feed itself first, while others gather around and petition him with outstretched hands. It seems that some of this meat sharing is to gain mating opportunities down the road, to bond with males, or to avoid the cost of fighting over a scrap of meat, a behavior known as *tolerated theft*. From one vantage point, it looks like hunter-gatherer sharing.

But then there's Thomas, the Cree man who knew his act would diminish his own profits but who would have felt "just dead inside" for not being generous. Human meat sharing is different from chimp meat sharing.

Human behavior is deeply ingrained through cultural conditioning, and if we violate our culture's rules, we feel soiled. This is adaptive because humans confront dilemmas: if I keep the meat, there's more for me and my kin, but then I'll be labeled stingy and no one will share with me when I need it. Cultural rules tell us how to behave even when we want to do otherwise. We punish those who break cultural rules, with everything from a stern glance to death, depending on the transgression. For humans, sharing goes beyond a simple tit-for-tat calculus. It's produced by cultural values instilled in us that make sure the calculus "comes out right," but it's linked to our cultural construction of the world. It results in "rules" of sharing, like those of the Gunwinggu, rather than in a mere instantaneous balancing of costs and benefits (which for selfish individuals could be costly in the long run).

So, when did hominins start sharing like humans? That's another difficult question to answer, but archaeologist Mary Stiner may have an answer.[10] When animals are butchered with a stone tool, the tool often cuts to the bone and leaves a telltale nick. If bones are well-preserved we can see these with the naked eye (and we can distinguish them from carnivore tooth marks or root etching). In her studies of animal bones from Qesem Cave in Israel, about 700,000 to 400,000 years old, Stiner found cut marks scattered over the bones and at random angles. These were different from cut marks left on bones in sites occupied much later by modern humans. There the cut marks concentrate on particular areas of the bone, those where a cut removes meat most easily. And the cut marks are at similar angles, suggesting the cutting was done by one person sitting in the same position relative to the carcass.

Stiner suggests that many hands processed the lower Paleolithic bones. Someone removed some meat, passed (or gave up) the limb to another, who removed another portion, and passed it on. It's not quite a free-for-all, but there's no evidence that sharing was coordinated or operated with a set of rules. Instead, the haphazard cut marks conjure an image that is more chimp-like than humanlike, reflecting social relationships negotiated in terms of who holds what resource—a hunk of meat, a possibility of mating or an alliance—and not by a set of rules that allows an elderly, crippled man back at camp to still get his share. Culture makes a difference in how sharing works. And at present we have no evidence for cultural rules of sharing, and no evidence of the capacity for culture, in the lower Paleolithic.

. . .

We can now turn to the most specifically physical manifestation of culture: the use of symbols.

To understand how symbols can track the appearance of the capacity for culture, we must remember that people are good at different things. Some are mechanically inclined and some are great athletes. Others are mathematicians, scientists, artists, or musicians. A lucky few excel in more than one area, some are mediocre in a bunch of subjects, and others are not especially good at anything.

This extends to the use of symbols. Some humans are excellent at the use and manipulation of symbols. I call them *supersymbolers*. These are individuals who can't seem to think of the world in terms of anything but symbols. Like my son who saw a swan in a weed, they see and hear things that others don't see or hear.

Duke Ellington, for example, wrote scores in New York City taxis because he heard music in the sounds of the city, just as Beethoven heard symphonies when he took walks in the forest. Bob Dylan's lyrics often make no sense, and yet when put to music, they communicate an emotion perfectly. Mozart, da Vinci, Picasso, O'Keefe, Dalí: all are artists who lie at the far, "creative" end of the bell curve of a population that is capable of thinking symbolically. And you know that the behavior of great artists often verges on the pathological. They are not "normal" people, but they produce a useful product and so they are not social outcasts. (People at the opposite end of the bell curve may include those with severe autism spectrum disorder, people who have trouble with symbols and who might only be able to understand another person's behavior literally.)

The point is that once a *population* is capable of thinking symbolically, we can expect some members of that population to be supersymbolers. And they will most likely produce symbols in the form of art because they wouldn't be able to help themselves.

George Bernard Shaw said that "without art, the crudeness of reality would make the world unbearable." Art is an effort to make sense of the world, to reconcile the crudeness of reality with a cultural vision of the world. The artist Norman Rockwell is sometimes ridiculed for his white-bread portrayals of American life at mid-twentieth century. But he was not painting scenes from his own life. Instead, he painted to reconcile the reality of life as he experienced it (divorce, depression, his second wife's death, rejection by the art community) with the construction of life that he had been taught. This is why art is often a tool of revolutionaries. It's why Mao Zedong said people should sing only patriotic songs. It's why Pete Seeger was blacklisted during the McCarthy era. And it's why Russia's President Putin put the female rock band Pussy Riot in prison.

Therefore, it appears likely that art first appeared in human history when our ancestors tried to reconcile the reality of life with their vision of what life should be like. This implies that they *had* a vision of what life should be like, a symbolically constructed vision of their world. They were thinking with several levels of intentionality: some people wanted others to know that they knew life was not going as they all expected it to go. Art signals the appearance of culture.

Remember that the capacity for culture is rooted in our brains. It arose through a genetic mutation, although we don't know what that mutation was. But since it's a mutation, it's possible for only one person in a population to have it. Imagine being that person, the only one who heard music in the wind, who saw swans in stems of grass, or who wondered about the similarity between a woven bag and crosshatching on shells or rocks. You couldn't explain yourself to anyone, or even to yourself. It would be a teenager's worst nightmare: you really would be different and no one would understand you.

We know that about 200,000 years ago, hominins were technologically savvy. They were fitting microliths, tiny stone blades, into wooden or bone hafts with glue made perhaps from the gum of acacia trees. Hominins who had the capacity to use that kind of technology and who were born supersymbolers, artists, might very well manipulate material things in their effort to reconcile their understanding of the world with their actual experience of the world.

Such concern with oneself might be why some of the earliest evidence of "symbolic" behavior comes in the form of pigment, maybe for tattoos or body paint, and shell beads. In South Africa, some people ground ochre (a natural earth pigment of hydrated iron oxide) into a red powder at least 70,000 years ago. Maybe it was only to create mastic to help bind stone tools into their wooden hafts, but one small piece of ochre from Blombos Cave on the coast of South Africa has a curious series of x's etched into its surface, whose tops, middles, and bottoms are connected with horizontal lines.[11] About the same time, other people in South Africa engraved ostrich eggshells with simple ladderlike designs.[12] There are seashell beads dated to about 80,000 years in Algeria and Morocco, 75,000 years in South Africa, and perhaps 100,000 years in the Near East.[13]

How would other hominins react to the first one to wear a shell necklace or to someone who covered his or her face or chest with lines of red pigment? Were they mystified? Freaked out? Intrigued? I'm going to guess "intrigued," in part because I know the end of the story and in part because of how chimps and bonobos treat oddities. Some primatologists today attach small, motion-sensitive cameras to trees so that they can study chimp behavior unobtrusively. But chimps are curious, and I've seen amusing footage of them smelling the camera, poking it, examining it closely, and "making faces" at it. Chimps do the same when researchers put marks or clothing on them. Middle Paleolithic hominins were intellectually far beyond chimps, and I expect they were curious about new things if for no other reason than from a technological point of view.

As a result, beads and pigment could have spread through a process known in evolutionary theory as the Baldwin effect. Middle Paleolithic hominins were obviously good social learners—that is evident in their technology. If those hominins could see that beads and body pigment attracted attention, possibly resulting in more mates or more food sharing, then some might have adopted the practice even if they did not have the genetic trait that had inspired the initial hominin's behavior. In this way, the genes responsible for the initial appearance of "symbolic" behavior could be maintained, at least at a low frequency, through the generations. Selection might not have worked strongly in favor of the trait, but it also would not have worked against it.

You might be thinking that this art, as I've described it, is unremarkable. Wouldn't we expect someone with an artistic capacity to create art as we see in the Upper Paleolithic (50,000–12,000 years ago) caves of France and Spain—paintings of aurochs (wild cattle), horses, and bison that make your jaw drop? Maybe . . . but what would artists produce if they had no artistic tradition to build on, if they had no community that could appreciate the effort, or if the necessary implements and materials were still in their infancy? Perhaps it was a Michelangelo who inscribed the small slab of ochre at Blombos Cave, but such simple engraving was all his or her tradition and technology at the time could muster.

Sometime after 200,000 years ago, at least some hominins had the mental capacity for culture, for creating a symbolic construction of life. The odd thing is that while beads and pigments appear around 80,000 years ago, instead of becoming more common through time, as we might expect, evidence of symbolic activity all but disappears about 65,000 years ago, and doesn't reappear until after 50,000 years ago. What happened?

We don't know. One hypothesis is that humans were nearly wiped off the face of the earth by a "nuclear winter" produced by the eruption of Mount Toba on the island of Sumatra about 74,000 years ago (one of the world's largest volcanic eruptions).[14] Extrapolating backwards from the distribution of genetic data around the globe, some geneticists calculate that the human population was substantially diminished sometime after 70,000 years ago.[15] In fact, if the breeding population was as small as some research estimates, then humans were on the brink of extinction. Such a small human population meant fewer supersymbolers to create new ideas and fewer people to carry on new traits. In small populations, and as a simple product of random chance, even good ideas may fail to be passed down from one generation to the next.

But the human population recovered and then grew, spreading throughout Africa, Europe, Asia, and eventually the rest of the world. Along the way these modern humans, *Homo sapiens,* replaced (or, at least in the case of Neanderthals, may have partially assimilated) those hominins who were descendants of previous migrations out of Africa. By at least 40,000 years ago, hominins were no longer just very clever apes; they were human.

. . .

The most dramatic expression of this fact comes from the Paleolithic rock art mentioned above, painted in European caves, starting soon after 40,000 years ago. For the most part, artists painted the animals of their world: aurochs, bears, lions, mammoths, rhinos, and horses as well as abstract designs of dots, hatched lines, and arched rainbowlike figures (oddly, human representations are rare). The art is sometimes found deep in caves, in places that were difficult to reach, especially with nothing more than a stone oil lamp or reed torch to light the way. It also includes carvings of bone, antler, and ivory (and of wood, no doubt, but wood does not preserve well).

Anthropologist David Lewis-Williams suggests the painted images in caves were what shamans saw in dreams and trances.[16] Shamans understand dreams and trances as a way to communicate with the deceased or spirits. They can induce trance through psychotropic drugs, deprivation, or physical exhaustion (for example, through dance). The interesting thing is that no matter which method they use, or what culture they come from, shamans all go through the same three stages of trance. They report first seeing particular shapes, including rainbows, dots, hatched designs, and squares. In the second stage, shamans see these abstract elements imposed over things from their daily life, such as animals. And in the third and deepest stage, shamans feel they are drawn into a dark swirling vortex and they cannot tell the difference between themselves and their vision; they become part of the hallucination.

Modern shamans from various cultures talk about the deepest stage of trance as "death" or as moving to "the other side." The deep recesses of caves might have been a place where Upper Paleolithic shamans sought to replicate the experience of trance and to reach the other side of existence. To do that, they had to think about that other side. Perhaps they saw their everyday life as a mere shadow of a "real" world that could be reached temporarily in dreams and trance and permanently in death. Rock art suggests that the artists who drew bison, lions, and mammoths on cave walls lived in a world that was not simply one of food, shelter, and reproduction, but one also of spirits, ancestors, and "other worlds." It was, in short, a symbolically constructed world.

Earlier hominins could probably talk competently about technology, bead making, tracking animals, and digging up tubers. I am less certain that they talked about life after death, the purpose of life, whether bears were actually people, what the dead ancestors would think of some course of action, or whether stars were the campfires of the deceased on their way to the next world. But cave art suggests that by at least 40,000 years ago, people communicated in a recognizably human way, almost certainly using metaphors and analogies. It's clear evidence of culture.

Is there any other evidence of the capacity for culture? Remember that culture is a set of ideas or beliefs that is shared by a group of people. It entails ideas about what men and woman should do, how children should be raised, whether the ancestors matter, what a reasonable goal in life is, how the aged should be treated, what should happen to wrongdoers, or why folks in the next valley seem a little weird. Knowing that such ideas are jointly held requires at least three and often four levels of intentionality: I have to know that you know that we both agree on what proper behavior is and that we know that the person over there knows this, too. This capacity is best manifested in behavior that we might gloss as "religion." When in human evolution do we see evidence for religion?

. . .

The origin of religion is another of anthropology's perplexing questions, and to answer it some scientists have adopted an evolutionary perspective.[17] Why should we consider religion from such a perspective? For the same reason that we think language is a product of evolution: it's everywhere. Individuals might reject religion, but all *cultures* contain religious thought (even where governments forbid it). Perhaps more than any other behavior, religion requires at least four levels of intentionality: I know that you know that we both understand that the spirits think we should act in a particular manner. How would this arise?

Some look to chimps for inspiration. Doing so, they find rare instances of male chimps that go "apeshit" when they hear thunder or encounter a roaring waterfall. This can happen when a male is alone, meaning that these are not displays done to demonstrate fearlessness to compatriots but are a response to something of obviously great "presence." I don't mean to compare anyone's religion to chimps waving branches at a waterfall. The significance of this behavior is that it suggests what kind of cognitive variation could have existed in an ancient hominin population—and evolution works with such variation.

One cognitive capacity is an *agent detection device,* a capacity that permits us to recognize that other actors have intentions. As social animals our goal is to know what those intentions are: Is another inclined to be friendly toward us? Are they angry, sad, or dangerous? This is a crucial capacity for those who live in groups.

But variation in cognitive capacities could create some individuals with an agent detection device that goes too far and who ascribe agency, the capacity to act with intention, to things like waterfalls, thunder, or trees. They could ascribe agency to an object if it appears to act (e.g., a mountain, by virtue of landslides) or if it "offers" itself as a useful piece of technology (like a nice chert stream cobble that could be fashioned into a tool). Those chimps who are inspired by a waterfall or lightning might be rare individuals who wonder (in a chimp way, whatever that is) what the waterfall or lightning intends to do with all its noise.

Some psychologists say that children are "natural theists" because when they acquire three levels of intentionality, they recognize that others have actions and that there is a mind behind those actions. They understand the mind as separate from the body and thus wonder where the mind goes when the body is no more. If grandmother's mind was not of her body, then where did it go when her body ceased to exist? This makes it seem reasonable, and comforting, to say "the really important part of grandma has not ceased to exist but has gone someplace else."

Knowing when religion appeared in human evolution means having some means of detecting it in the archaeological record. Although the surface structures of religions are different, just like languages, they contain some similar structural elements. One of these is an understanding that there is an existence beyond mortal life and that death is the portal to it. This makes intentional burial ritual, a sending-off of a person to the next world, a crucial part of religious practices. And the nice thing about rituals is that they often leave physical traces, making archaeologists happy.

When does burial ritual first appear? Many remains of early hominins—of the australopithecines, for example—are found in what archaeologists call secondary deposits, such as stream sediments; those remains are not where they were originally deposited, and so we can't look to them for evidence of burial ritual.

But chimps, as our closest evolutionary relative, might provide a clue.[18] Chimps are often fascinated, confused, and upset by their dead compatriots. Chimps might appreciate that a fellow chimp climbing a tree intends to play, but what is his intention when he falls to the ground and lies still? Some female chimps carry their dead infants around for weeks, as the little creature's body rots and falls apart. Others poke at a dead body, sniff it, and lift the motionless hands. Sometimes they drag it off into tall grass; perhaps that's their burial "ritual," or maybe they just want to remove the source of confusion. In any case, there is nothing in the archaeology of the australopithecines and early *Homo* to say that they treated the dead any differently than do chimps today.

We have better evidence for Neanderthals (Neanderthals made use of caves, which are good for preservation). Some Neanderthals were clearly buried in shallow pits, but the evidence for burial ritual is not very convincing.[19] One burial from Iraq's Shanidar Cave contained clumps of pollen from a variety of flowers, suggesting that entire flower heads were laid in the grave. But were they laid there by the hands of a grieving Neanderthal? Perhaps, but we can't discount that the flower heads were put there by a rodent (the Persian jird) who found the loose earth of the burial a handy place to dig its burrow and store its food, which is, in fact, flower heads. Archaeology can be quite frustrating.

But by 40,000 or 50,000 years ago the evidence for burial ritual is unequivocal: *Homo sapiens* laid out a body in a consistent, no doubt culturally prescribed manner (e.g., in a fetal position), sometimes covering it with red ochre powder, and laying tools, personal goods, and food beside it. Although some burials contain no grave goods, enough do that we suppose those without goods lost them to poor preservation (or maybe no one liked those particular folks). So our best evidence for human burial ritual, a sign of a belief in an afterlife, of religion, and of culture, appears in the last 50,000 years, at the same time that art becomes widespread.

The human capacity for culture entails several capabilities that all came together between 200,000 and 50,000 years ago. In evolutionary time, that's fast. Why should the capacity for culture have become so prevalent so quickly?

. . .

We assume culture is adaptive. By that, we mean that a shared understanding of the "meaning" of the world must have motivated behaviors that increased the reproductive fitness of those hominins with the capacity for culture over those who lacked such a capacity.

What is probably at work here is a selective process that operates at the level of a group rather than at the level of individuals. Culture creates a group because people identify with others who share their beliefs about the world. Those beliefs are shorthand for whether someone will think about the world as you do, and consequently for whether that someone can be trusted. If a person speaks your language, shares meat in the same way you do, enjoys the same music, and shares your religion, you are more likely to assume that he or she will participate in the give-and-take of life in a manner that you consider to be fair (and thus beneficial for you). In other words, culture is a crucial tool in cooperative relationships.

What are the advantages of culture as a tool of cooperation?

Here's an odd fact: Culture makes relations with others simultaneously personal and not personal. Anyone who has traveled overseas knows the feeling of camaraderie that exists among expatriates, even those who have just met. Working in a foreign culture and language can be exhausting, and encountering a compatriot is often a relief, for that person is someone with whom you can talk easily and quickly, and whose every movement and gesture is familiar and easy to interpret correctly.

But culture can also make relationships between people not personal. Imagine a Gunwinggu man butchering a kangaroo. He puts too much meat on his own pile and not enough on that of his mother-in-law. His mother-in-law may not have to fight for herself; someone else may point out that she has been shortchanged. And it's not that the person is complaining on behalf of the mother-in-law. That person is simply pointing out that someone has broken the rule, he has done something that isn't right because, well, it's not the way Gunwinggu do things. This isn't one person challenging another as much as it is one person reminding another (and everyone else present) of how a proper Gunwinggu, of how a proper person, operates. If the butcher continues to be stingy, he pays a social price, because even those people who watched silently now know that this man is not a proper Gunwinggu, is not to be trusted, and is not to be shared with.

By becoming deeply ingrained, cultural norms become their own police force. How many of us have been tempted to do something wrong but have not succumbed because we listened to that little voice in the back of our head. We avoid violating cultural norms because, like Thomas, the Cree hunter, we would feel "just dead inside." Men in battle have taken deadly risks to save their friends. When asked why they did so, they often say that they couldn't have lived with themselves if they had not—so what was there to lose? This is culture at work, and language supports culture. I don't have to witness a Gunwinggu hunter's stinginess, since gossip will ensure that everyone knows he's stingy and someone to avoid. Coupled with language, culture is a low-cost way to enforce cooperation.

And those who are cooperative are rewarded. Think back to our discussion of sharing. You can tussle over meat, or you can "generously" give it away. This benefits those receiving the meat, but it also benefits the giver. Compiling data from six modern foraging societies, anthropologist Eric Smith found that men who were good hunters and who were generous have more offspring than men who are poor hunters (and who consequently have little with which to be generous).[20] Men who are good hunters can obviously feed their children better. But Smith also found that generous hunters were able to marry early and to attract wives with similar food-producing capabilities. Their generosity also created debts and alliances with people who then watched over their offspring. And in their old age, generous men found themselves surrounded by helpful family members and friends.[21]

The generous hunter benefitted, but so did the people around him. The tug-of-war we experience between selfish and selfless desires suggests that we calculate the benefits of both. Selfish behavior has its benefits, but in a cultural environment, so does *selfless* behavior.

If the capacity for culture allows for the creation of a symbolically constructed universe, and if humans can see that generosity is a good thing, then generosity could become reinforced and made more frequent through culture. Good hunters would continue to have high rates of reproductive fitness, but so would the people who gather around them and who, through culture, have a way to ensure generosity. In this way, cultural groups of hominins could outcompete noncultural ones.

. . .

Somewhere in Africa, perhaps in a cave along the continent's southern coast, probably between 200,000 and 50,000 years ago, the second beginning, the emergence of culture, occurred. Sitting on your chair in space, you notice two things. First, technology is no longer the same over vast stretches of space and time. No, it changes much more rapidly now, and different styles and different types of tools appear in different environments. No single technology covers the vast temporal and geographic reign of Oldowan or Acheulian tools. Technologies seem to be suited to a local environment's particular demands, but some differences are a matter of style. You are witnessing the development of regional cultures, each with its own way of making tools, telling stories, sharing food, marrying, worshipping, and burying the dead. This happens everywhere that *Homo sapiens* sets foot. This is evidence of different *cultures,* something that is impossible without the capacity for *culture.*

Hominins entered the Pleistocene world as creatures unable to appreciate a blazing sunset as anything more than a sign they should retreat for the night. They would have been unmoved by a haiku's few lines, have had no feeling of loneliness at the sight of Edward Hopper's *Nighthawks,* or been moved to action by a Bob Dylan or Pete Seeger protest song. But sometime after 200,000 years ago, and certainly by 50,000 years ago, we were human, fully capable of doing all these things. The way things were three million years ago was nothing like the way they were 50,000 years ago. The more things changed, the more things changed. And that process wasn't about to stop.

CHAPTER 5

Bread and Beer

The Beginning of Agriculture

The present contains nothing more than the past, and what
is found in the effect was already in the cause.
—Henri L. Bergson

From your perch in space you don't see much significant change across
the globe after 50,000 or 60,000 years ago. . . until about 10,000 B.C.
Then you have to pay attention. The third beginning entails the appearance of domesticated plants: wheat and barley in the Near East, millet
in northern China and rice in southern China and Southeast Asia, maize
and squash in Mexico, potatoes and quinoa in the highland Andes, millet and sorghum in central Africa. That's only the start, however, for the
first domesticated plants are later joined by peas and lentils, tomatoes,
fruit trees, grapes, bananas, and yams, among others.

Another new item you see is domesticated animals. Dogs have
already been domesticated; in fact, they had been skulking around
hunter-gatherer fires by at least 13,000 B.C. and perhaps as early as
33,000 B.C.[1] But soon after 10,000 B.C., man's best friend is accompanied by cattle, sheep, goats, pigs, llamas, horses, and turkeys.[2] Most of
these animals are Old World species. Domesticated animals are rare in
the New World (prior to European colonization). There are llamas in
highland South America—used as beasts of burden and as a source of
wool and meat—along with guinea pigs (for food; they are lousy beasts
of burden), and people in northern Mexico and the American Southwest keep turkeys. But the large game native to the New World such as
deer, pronghorn, and bison are poor candidates for domestication. For
whatever reason, New World game doesn't contain the genetic varieties
to create docile critters that can be bossed around. You won't see a

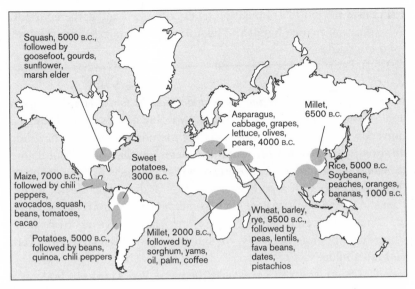

FIGURE 2. Where and when some of the world's major domesticated plants first appeared.

rancher today driving tame bison down a country lane as dairy farmers do with Holsteins.

You also see that communities are suddenly quite different from the hunter-gatherer camps of the preceding tens of millennia. Their number and size reflect a rapidly growing population. The houses are more substantial, and the communities are replete with features that reflect permanence—cookhouses, storerooms, wells, plazas, and cemeteries. Plants and animals that formerly had lived in particular geographic locales spread across continents. Maize, for example, originated in southern Mexico (see figure 2), but by the time Europeans arrived in the New World, it had spread south into the Andes and the Amazon basin and north as far as southeastern Canada.

After tens of thousands of years as hunter-gatherers, many people became agriculturalists. Eventually, that led to today, when the world's seven and a half billion people depend on a billion metric tons of maize, 738 million metric tons of rice, 711 million metric tons of wheat, 375 million metric tons of potatoes, 143 million metric tons of barley, 25 million metric tons of millet, 24 million metric tons of oats, and 17 million metric tons of rye.[3] The hunting and gathering lifeway had served the human species well for tens of thousands of years. But today, only a fraction of the world's population relies on hunted and gathered foods. Why did this change happen? This question has puzzled archaeology for a long time.

. . .

In the film *Indiana Jones and the Kingdom of the Crystal Skull,* Indiana and his son escape from Soviet agents by riding a motorcycle through a university library (in fact, Yale's Sterling Memorial Library). They slide on their bike beneath a row of tables, then right themselves, but before they roar off, a student, so absorbed in his reading as to be unaware of the action, asks Professor Jones a question. Indiana was clearly preoccupied, but the film's writers knew something about university faculty: we always answer a student's question. And the writers also knew something about archaeology, for Indiana referred the student to Vere Gordon Childe.

Chances are you will never hear the name Vere Gordon Childe in a movie again, but he was a real person. Born in 1892 in Australia, he was educated in archaeology at Oxford University. Archaeology wasn't much of a paying profession back then, so Childe first worked for the Australian Labour Party. That experience probably solidified his political views, which were openly socialist, a fact reflected in his approach to prehistory. He eventually gained a post at the University of Edinburgh and, in 1947, became director of the Institute of Archaeology at University College London. He retired in 1957 and, sadly, committed suicide that same year by leaping off a cliff in Australia's Blue Mountains.[4]

Childe was a brilliant thinker and synthesizer of archaeological data. His books provided a rhyme and reason for the cultural changes recorded in the archaeology of Europe and southwest Asia. In *Man Makes Himself,* he proposed one of the first explanations of the origins of agriculture.[5]

Like many thinkers of his time, Childe surmised that history recorded progress, humankind's struggle to move ahead, to make life more civilized, more moral. As a socialist, he also believed change occurred through revolutions, but not the violent, storm-the-Bastille kind (he was personally a very gentle man). Instead, he thought revolutions occurred through ideas, ideas that would be implemented when the light bulb came on in the proper circumstances, since those ideas would produce the greatest good for the greatest number.

Childe assumed that agriculture was one such idea, so for him the only questions were where, when, and how. Childe decided agriculture had appeared as a result of the dry climate of the terminal Ice Age in the Near East, where wild wheat and barley are found. He thought the idea for agriculture would have caught on where plants and humans were forced into close association, and, given the dry climate, he thought that had to be someplace where water and life were concentrated, as in the Nile valley, where you can go from verdant fields to desolate desert in a single step.

Childe reasoned that because people and plants lived cheek by jowl along the Nile, "some genius" would eventually figure out that plants came from seeds. Likewise, he thought someone would eventually see the wisdom of controlling animals. Thus, some plants and animals came to be domesticated, dependent on humans for their propagation.

Childe got some things right. The Near East is the hearth of the world's earliest agriculture, and people began growing food there at the tail end of the Ice Age. But he was wrong about where it first occurred; it turns out it wasn't along the Nile but near the native stands of wild wheat and barley in the mountains of Syria, Turkey, and Iraq.

He was also wrong about the cause. Becoming a farmer requires more than realizing that plants come from seeds. Many modern hunter-gatherers trade with agriculturalists; they understand agriculture and yet they do not till fields. Other hunter-gatherers were agriculturalists who "returned" to hunting and gathering. The Lakota, for example (you may know them as the Sioux), were once farmers of the western Great Lakes. They were pushed onto the plains in the late seventeenth century by the Ojibwa, who had acquired guns from French fur trappers. About the same time, the Spanish entered the American Southwest from Mexico with horses. The Lakota captured some runaways and, in the mid-eighteenth century, became the horse-mounted bison hunters that we erroneously think of as timeless denizens of the American Plains.

If Childe was wrong, if simple knowledge of plant and animal domestication doesn't explain agriculture, what does? To answer that question, we have to back up in time a little.

. . .

As I mentioned in the last chapter, when *Homo sapiens* moved out of Africa sometime after 70,000 years ago, they recolonized parts of the world that were already occupied by some hominin species, including Neanderthals in Europe. Neanderthals have had a bum rap ever since they were first discovered in Germany's Neander Valley in 1856.[6] Due to mistakes and prejudices, Neanderthals became the poster child for stoop-shouldered, beetle-browed, drooling troglodytes.

The image is wrong. Neanderthals' bodies were adapted to the cold; and, in fact, they couldn't have been stupid, since they survived in a rough Ice Age environment populated by nasty creatures such as cave bears. Still, they disappeared from the scene about 40,000 years ago, suspiciously after having *Homo sapiens* as their neighbors for some 5,000 years. We don't know how modern humans replaced them. It's clear that Neanderthals and *Homo sapiens* interbred, because those of European descent retain some Neanderthal genetic material (about 1–3 percent). In Asia, *Homo sapiens* also replaced another group of early humans that paleoanthropologists call Denisovans (we know less about the Denisovans because we've learned everything about them genetically from one bone of a young girl's pinky finger).[7] Paleoanthropologists are still reading this story from the bones.

What matters is that hominins with the capacity for culture eventually dominated the world after 50,000 years ago. They colonized Europe and Asia, pausing only while the glaciers that covered Scandinavia and northern Russia retreated. They survived the vast steppes and forests of Siberia and Mongolia and, by 30,000 years ago, were living on the north shores of Russia (they retreated during another pulse of the Ice Age but returned about 18,000 years ago as the last glacial period waned).

From far eastern Russia, humans crossed the Bering Strait when a glacial period lowered sea level and connected the continents, and arrived in North America by at least 13,000 B.C.[8] They traveled south, either along the western coast or through a corridor between the two massive ice sheets that spread across Canada, one over the Canadian Rockies and the other centered on Hudson Bay. Once south of the glaciers, they spread across the United States and by 11,000 B.C., at least, were in Central and South America. Compared to the Old World, the New World—from Alaska to Tierra del Fuego—was colonized in the blink of an eye.

Others in Asia had migrated south through the tropical forests, down the Indonesian archipelago. With boats, they had migrated across open water, island-hopping to New Guinea and arriving down under in Australia about 50,000 years ago.

In brief, from our perch in the stratosphere, we witness a global human migration driven by slow population growth, and by 10,000 B.C. nearly the entire world is colonized by hunter-gatherers. *Homo sapiens* was a colonizing species, and movement was an essential component of the hunting and gathering adaptation. What happened when there was no place left to move?[9]

. . .

Hunter-gatherers never meant to become agriculturalists. No hunter woke up one morning and said "I think I'll take up farming, maybe some wheat and arugula." No, hunter-gatherers became agriculturalists while trying to become better at what they already did so well—hunting and gathering. Does that sound paradoxical?

Domesticated plants obviously come from wild plants. We know what some of those ancestral plants were, and, frankly, they aren't that impressive. Maize, for example, comes from *teocintle*, a tall tropical grass that grows wild in southern Mexico. But teocintle's seeds are tiny, and its "cob" is smaller than your pinky; it's nothing like the genetic mutants that come out of Nebraska's cornfields. No one would look at teocintle and say, "Someday this plant will feed much of the world's population and help produce biofuel." But foragers in southern Mexico did harvest teocintle, and eventually they turned it into the maize that we know. Why that happened has to do with how nomadic hunter-gatherers decide what to eat and when to move.

Hunter-gatherers are just like you and me, only different. They have the same minds as anyone else in the world, and they make decisions with the same capacities and using the same principles; they just do that under different circumstances. They weigh the costs and benefits of the different possibilities available to achieve some goal and, as one principle, opt for those choices that will provide them with the biggest bang for their buck; in the case of food, that would be the greatest number of calories for the least amount of work. This is the basis of a class of theoretical models known as *optimal foraging models,* the most widely applied of which is the Diet Breadth Model, or DBM. Although the model is simple, its implications are far-reaching.

Imagine foragers walking through the forest. When those foragers encounter food, such as berries or tubers, or a sign of food, such as fresh deer tracks, they decide whether to pursue it, or to ignore it and keep searching. If they choose to pursue the food, to pick the berries or track the deer, they pass up the chance to search for other, perhaps better, foods. But if they ignore the immediate option, they might miss a chance to bring home something rather than nothing. How do they decide?

The DBM assumes that foragers aim to select the suite of foods that provides them with the highest average rate of return. This is either so they can gather as much food as possible during the entire working day (e.g., when they are putting up food stores for the winter), so they can gather the minimum needed and devote time to other important things (e.g., trading, socializing, educating children, or religious affairs), or, if predators are a problem, so they can return to the safety of camp as soon as possible.

To implement the DBM, we need to know three things about a hunter-gatherer's possible foods: (1) How many calories does each resource provide? For hunter-gatherers, we need information on foods that standard government dietary measures don't include, such as wild sego lily bulbs, crayfish, bear meat, hedgehogs, grasshoppers, whitebark pine nuts, and wichetty grubs (eaten in Aboriginal Australia; they're not bad). We acquire this information by sending samples to a lab, the same ones that produce the dietary labels on packaged food. (2) We also need to know how abundant a food is across a landscape, since abundance tells us how hard it is to find that food. (3) Finally, we need to know how much time it takes to harvest a food and convert it into something edible once it's found. Some foods, such as berries, are easy to collect and consume. Others, such as acorns, require a lot of processing before they are edible. We refer to this last piece of information as a food's *return rate*.

Anthropologists and archaeologists have actually calculated return rates for many food resources. Sometimes we've done this through ethnographic research, by observing modern hunter-gatherers and recording their behavior; at other times we've gathered the necessary data through experimental work.

Archaeologist Steven Simms was one of the first to conduct experimental foraging to determine return rates.[10] It took an archaeologist to do this because Simms wanted to use an optimal foraging model in his research in the Great Basin of the western United States, but no one there today gathers wild foods using aboriginal technology. So he had to do it himself. Using historical accounts, he reconstructed the technology used to harvest various plant foods, then he practiced until he was good enough to produce reliable return rates.

One of the foods Simms gathered was ricegrass. He did so in a manner similar to the way the Great Basin Shoshone and Paiute used to collect it, using a woven instrument that looks like a Ping-Pong paddle and a tightly woven basket. Walking through a stand of ricegrass in July, he hit the seed heads with his paddle, knocking them into the basket that he carried in his other hand. He then ground the seeds into flour, using traditional stone grinding tools. After 41 minutes he had 96 grams of ricegrass seed flour. Ricegrass contains about 2.74 calories per gram, so its return rate is 2.74 cal/g × 96 g/41 min = 6.41 cal/min or 385 cal/hr. Return rates can vary from as low as 100 cals/hour to as high as several hundred thousand cals/hour (although those are rare), and the rates are affected by technology and season.

Given information on the densities, nutrition, and return rates of foods, the DBM tells us which combination of foods foragers would select if they wanted to maximize their return. In brief, the DBM tells foragers: when you encounter a food, take it *if* that food's return rate is higher than the expected average return rate of this environment, taking all possible resource search and harvesting costs into account. You might ask, how the heck can anyone calculate that? One of the wonders of the human mind is that we make all kinds of mathematical calculations without actually knowing math. The forager uses his or her experience to decide whether taking an encountered resource is a good use of time. The DBM simply models that process mathematically and, tested against some modern hunter-gatherers, such as South America's Ache and Africa's Hadza, does a pretty good job of predicting reality. Just like the rest of us, hunter-gatherers try to make the best use of their time.

Now here's the strange part. The wild ancestors of the world's major agricultural plants—teocintle, wild rice, wheat, barley, and millet—are small seeds, and small seeds generally have low return rates. How did low-return-rate foods come to support a world population of over seven billion people?

. . .

To answer that question, let's consider one low-return-rate food that did *not* go on to a glorious future—the acorn.

If you've never tried acorns, pick one up sometime (especially from a red oak), break the outer shell, pick out the nut meat, pop it in your mouth, and start chewing. But be warned: your mouth will go dry instantly. And if you eat a handful, you'll become ill, and you'll wonder how ancient Californian hunter-gatherers could have eaten acorn meal all winter. The reason is that someone, probably through a fortuitous accident or trial and error, discovered that acorns can be eaten if you remove their tannic acid. To do this, you gather the acorns, break open the shells, and remove the nut meat. Pound the nut meat into something like cold, lumpy, mashed potatoes, and spread it over green leaves. Then heat water, and pour it over the mash, several times. That will leach out the tannic acid. Once dried, the mash can be stored for the winter. It's not especially appetizing, but it's edible.

Processing acorns takes considerable time, so its return rate is low. Yet acorns were a significant part of aboriginal diet in California when Europeans first arrived in the sixteenth century. Why?

Archaeology tells us that California's aborigines didn't always rely on acorns. In fact, they shifted to a diet high in acorns late in prehistory. Acorns weren't their first choice in the San Fernando Valley supermarket. But California has a relatively benign climate and was rich in hunted and gathered foods. As a result, the population there grew . . . and grew. For nomadic hunter-gatherers, this creates a problem.

As hunter-gatherers forage around their camp, they deplete their food resources; the longer they stay in one place, the further from camp they must forage. Foragers can travel only about ten kilometers from camp before they must stay out overnight, because you can't walk more than a twenty-kilometer round trip and also do much work in a day. Men might stay out overnight when hunting, but women, often carrying children, return to camp at night (incidentally, this means women's foraging determines when camp is moved). In any case, the longer hunter-gatherers stay in a camp, the more time they spend searching for food, and the lower their overall return rate.

Hunter-gatherers balance an ever-declining return against the cost of moving to a new camp. Many things affect the cost of moving to a new camp, including the distance to the next camp (which might be dictated by water or firewood), terrain, weather, or even insects (without bug spray, they have a bigger effect than you might think). Arctic hunters, for example, might stay in their current camp and hunt at longer distances if the distance to the next stand of trees (which provide firewood) is far.[11]

Hunter-gatherers can also move to a new camp only if someone is not already there. And as population density increases, so too does the likelihood that someone will have already occupied the next camp on the landscape. In that case, the hunter-gatherers have two choices: either push others from a desired piece of land or stay where you are and *diversify your diet*. The first option is risky, since you might lose the fight. The second option arises from the Diet Breadth Model. If you've depleted the high-ranked resources, then you must add lower-ranked resources to your diet. And these will be resources that may be abundant but that entail higher processing costs, like acorns.

As California's prehistoric population grew, some hunter-gatherers settled down and turned to acorns for food. So why didn't acorns have the same history as wheat, maize, or rice? One way to overcome a food's low return rate is to increase a plant's productivity or abundance, grow denser stands of wheat, or select the right maize kernels to grow ever larger cobs. But it's difficult to make California's hillsides produce more oak trees or to make the individual trees produce more or larger acorns. California's native inhabitants could have planted trees, but they would not have seen the benefit for years. And people tend to discount the future since they need to eat today. The plants that *did* go on to become the workhorses of modern diet were mostly annuals, plants that have a relatively short time between planting and harvest—ninety days in the case of maize—and that could be made more productive through intentional human selection. And so today we eat wheat bread, rice cakes, and corn muffins rather than acorns.

To see how the transition from hunting and gathering happened, let's consider one of the best studied instances of agricultural origins, that of the Near East.[12]

. . .

My first encounter with the Near East was Cairo. If you've never visited Cairo, you should definitely put it on your bucket list. It's not as beautiful as Paris or as cosmopolitan as London, but for sheer energy, it's without rival. The streets are packed with everything from tractor-trailers to donkey carts. The *souks* are filled with spices, fish, freshly butchered goat, produce, and, for the tourists, every kind of pharaoh-related kitsch and pseudo-hieroglyphic trinket you can imagine. And the city is packed with people. Vendors haul loads through the streets, shop keepers invite you in for tea (that's the first step in a purchase), men kneel on prayer rugs and recite prayers. As someone who grew up in a rural area, I always marvel at how people can live under such packed, noisy conditions and not go insane.

The Near East was not always so crowded. Only 15,000 years ago, in fact, it was lightly inhabited, and everyone lived as nomadic hunter-gatherers throughout the "fertile crescent," that arc of highlands running from Palestine, Israel, and Jordan, through Lebanon, and into Syria, southern Turkey, and northern Iraq and Iran. This is the home of wild wheat and barley, as well as of wild goats, sheep, and cattle.

Childe was on the right track when he pointed to climate as key to the origins of agriculture. He was thinking of the climate changes that marked the end of the Pleistocene. Popularly known as the Ice Age, the Pleistocene lasted from 2.6 million to about 12,000 years ago.[13] It was a time when a colder climate allowed massive sheets of ice, up to two miles thick in places, to accumulate over vast portions of the northern hemisphere and in mountain valleys.[14]

The ice sheets advanced and retreated more than one hundred times during the Pleistocene. When the ice advanced, it took huge amounts of water out of circulation, so much so that sea level fell by up to 150 meters relative to today's shorelines. During times of glacial advance, the world was colder, but it was also drier.

As the earth warmed at the end of the Pleistocene and the glaciers retreated, water was freed up, and dry places became wetter. And, for reasons that are still unclear, atmospheric carbon dioxide increased. If you recall high school biology, plants take in carbon dioxide through photosynthesis, strip off the carbon they need for growth, and expel the oxygen. So at the end of the Pleistocene there was more water and more carbon dioxide; what more could plants ask for? Humans probably had the capacity for agriculture a long time before the end of the Pleistocene, but it was only at the end of the Pleistocene that the planets were aligned: hunter-gatherers had filled the globe and could no longer solve food problems by moving, and the environment was primed for a new solution.

Starting about 14,500 B.C., the Near East became wetter, with plenty of sunlight and carbon dioxide. Environmental productivity increased, and so did the human population. In fact, the human population had been growing, beginning some 50,000 years ago or so, at a rate of perhaps 0.04 percent per year. That's very slow, but at that rate a very small population could grow into a world population in the early nineteenth century of one billion.[15] Even modest population growth eventually filled up all available hunting and gathering niches.

By about 13,000 B.C., one of those shifts in material culture occurred in the Near East that makes archaeologists take notice and name the era. We call the period of time from 12,500 to 9500 B.C. in the Near East the *Natufian*. Its characteristics include semisubterranean stone-walled houses, storage bins, and large grinding stones—odd features for a hunter-gatherer settlement.

The Natufians did exactly what I would expect hunter-gatherers to do when confronted with a crowded environment. If the cost of moving means treading on the toes of others, then one response, probably the first one, is to simply grab a good spot on the landscape and stay there. It's similar to the game of musical chairs, only some of the chairs are more comfortable than others. The first places taken are the best places, and in the Fertile Crescent, the best places were those next to stands of wild cereals. And that's where Natufian foragers settled.

This adaptation worked fine for awhile, and then, to phrase it in technical terms, the stuff hit the fan.

. . .

The Natufians lived in a warming environment, but about 10,900 B.C., earth suddenly returned to cold conditions—in fact, to glacial conditions. And those conditions lasted for a thousand or more years during a climate period known as the Younger Dryas.[16] Why did a warming climate suddenly switch to a cold climate?

The answer has to do with ocean currents. Like a global conveyor belt, the ocean's water circulates in massive surface and subsurface currents.[17] One surface current, which includes the Gulf Stream, carries warm tropical water northward in the Atlantic Ocean. As the westerly winds move across this current, they pick up warm water and subsequently warm Europe. Scotland is at the same latitude as the middle of Hudson Bay, yet the Scots, unlike the Inuit, can grow oats because the ocean current warms the air. How much this current can warm Europe is a product of how far it penetrates into the North Atlantic, and how far it penetrates into the North Atlantic is partly due to how much fresh water flows into the North Atlantic. As tropical waters move northward, they become more saline as sea ice forms (salt is forced out as sea water freezes). Saline water is heavier than fresh water, and so when saline water encounters fresh water, it slides below it to the ocean's depths. What does this have to do with the Younger Dryas?

As the North American glaciers receded at the end of the Pleistocene, the meltwater formed Lake Agassiz over most of the province of Manitoba and parts of Saskatchewan and Ontario. Lake Agassiz was huge, the size of today's Black Sea and much larger than the Great Lakes combined. The hypothesis is that this lake drained suddenly, perhaps as a result of collapsed ice dams. The lake's fresh water drained to the north, perhaps via the Mackenzie River, and gushed into the Arctic Ocean, where it eventually reached the North Atlantic through the Fram Strait on the east side of Greenland. Deep sea sediment cores record this flood, which probably went on for decades. A concurrent melting of the Scandinavian ice sheet may have contributed additional fresh water.

This rapid influx of fresh water into the North Atlantic changed the ocean's circulation. The saltier water coming up from the south was driven down at a more southerly latitude than before the Lake Agassiz flood. As a result, the westerly winds picked up cold instead of warm water and put Europe and northern Asia into a deep freeze. Glaciers returned, locking up water, and the Near East dried up. Ironically, climatic warming produced climatic cooling. (The movie *The Day after Tomorrow* makes use of the same climatic trigger, only it plays fast and loose with the science and speeds the process up unrealistically and, since it's Hollywood, violently.)

In the Near East, the Younger Dryas pulled the rug out from under the human population, and produced a more variable climate, warm and dry some years, cool and wet in others. The Natufians needed to increase their environment's productivity, and so along the west wing of the Fertile Crescent, some became part-time cultivators of wild cereals, probably beginning with rye and later wheat and barley. Other groups, those who lost the game of musical chairs, remained hunter-gatherers and became nomadic, moving in the vacant areas among the sedentary villages.

Sometime between 9500 and 8500 B.C., a period of time that Near Eastern archaeologists label Pre-Pottery Neolithic A, people built larger villages (including one at the Biblical site of Jericho) and cultivated rye, emmer wheat, barley, and oats, along with vetch, peas, and lentils (see figure 2). This is when truly domesticated versions of some plants appeared. Later, between 8500 and 6500 B.C., the Pre-Pottery Neolithic B period, fully fledged agricultural villages appear, with einkorn wheat, chickpeas, vetch, lentils, and fava beans added to the menu; inhabitants of these villages were also domesticating sheep and goats (and later, cattle and pigs). Near Eastern cuisine is rooted in the economic changes that population growth and climate change wrought on local populations at the end of the Ice Age.

In order for agriculture to happen, certain changes had to occur in the genetic composition of plant communities. Sometimes humans directed those changes. For example, people most likely retained seeds from wheat plants with multiple rows (wild wheat usually has two seed rows; domesticated wheat, six). In doing so, they selected for more productive plants. But selection also happened unintentionally. For example, wild wheat tends to have a brittle rachis, the part of the wheat plant that holds the seed to the stem. A few plants have a strong rachis, which holds onto the seeds tightly; those with brittle rachises let go more easily. In the process of gathering, many of the seeds with the genes for a weak rachis were lost as plants were pulled up or sickled from fields. As a result, planted fields came to contain predominantly strong-rachis wheat.

Wheat seeds are also encased in a strong glume, or husk, which humans must remove in order to digest the seeds. Early domesticated wheat was productive, but it had high processing costs since the wheat had to be threshed. It took one thousand to two thousand years, but eventually humans created something close to the wheat we know today. This probably first happened in southeastern Turkey.[18]

We also learn something about how agriculture arose when we realize that one of the first crops was barley, which appears in a domesticated form during the Pre-Pottery Neolithic A. You might be tempted to say it was for beer, and indeed, beer was one of the first things made with barley, but the real reason may be that barley withstands warm, dry climates and grows well in poor, somewhat saline soils. If the musical chair you happened to be left with was not so favorable, you would try to make your land more productive, and that could mean growing barley.

. . .

Similar processes happened in other parts of the world. In southern Mexico, maize was the domesticated version of teocintle (see figure 2). In fact, genetic detective work by John Doebley places the origin of maize in the Central Balsas River Valley of southwestern Mexico about 7000 B.C.[19] Teocintle is hardly a plant on which to build a civilization, and it probably took hunter-gatherers a few thousand years of selection to create the plant that we recognize today as maize by intentionally selecting for large seed sizes and multiple seed rows. Unlike the Near East, this did not occur in the context of sedentary villages, which would appear later in Mexico. Instead, it appears that these Central American hunter-gatherers slowly added cultivated food to their dietary portfolio. Maize agriculture perhaps began as a minor component of the diet, with hunter-gatherers planting seeds along wet river banks, but not concerning themselves if the crop failed.

Hunter-gatherers did this with many plants. In Mexico and Peru, squash and bottle gourd (grown as containers, not as food; the seeds can be eaten but flesh is thin and bitter) were grown as early as 8000 B.C. (genetic data suggest the original plants may have come from Asia, having floated over on currents). Forager/farmers in the eastern U.S. domesticated a native squash about 5000 B.C., and streamside plants such as sunflower, sumpweed (marsh elder), and goosefoot about 3000 B.C., and later, knotweed and maygrass. Some of these are "weedy" plants that do well in disturbed habitats. As people cut down trees along river banks for construction or firewood, those banks supported more of the weedy plants. As the plants became more abundant, their return rates increased to the point where they became worth exploiting on a regular basis. Intentional selection for larger seed sizes as well as intentional planting also helped.

But while many are called, few are chosen. Those plants cultivated in the eastern U.S. did not go on to glorious careers (ever seen sumpweed in the supermarket?). But some, such as teocintle and wild wheat and barley, among others, happened to be genetically "plastic" enough that a clever selective agent, such as a hungry human, could eventually turn them into productive, high-return-rate foods.

People's intentional manipulation of these fortuitous plants became the primary vehicle for selection and plant evolution.[20] Ancient farmers worked with strains of maize, rice, potatoes, and so on the same way that a modern farmer might. They intentionally increased the return rate of their crops by increasing seed size and plant density through selective breeding, and through technological innovations such as the sickle, the plow, irrigation, terracing, and fertilizer. Eventually, they produced plants that became the focus of subsistence. At that point, an agricultural community was born. Ensuing population growth led some of those agriculturalists to radiate outward with their plants. Maize spread throughout Mexico by 5500 B.C., and was soon joined by squashes, beans, and tomatoes; settled villages appear by 4000 B.C. Maize agriculture then expanded to the north and south. In the eastern United States, it replaced the small, streamside plants about A.D. 700–1000, and along with potatoes, maize became an important crop in the central Andes after 3000 B.C.

Meanwhile, in China, domesticated millet and rice appeared about 8000 B.C., and millet and sorghum in sub-Saharan Africa (millet about 2000 B.C.; cattle, goat, and sheep domestication, perhaps around 4000 B.C., preceded plant domestication there; see figure 2). The timing varied around the world, but eventually many people transitioned to agriculture from hunting and gathering after 10,000 years ago. Sitting on your perch in space, you see a world dominated by hunter-gatherers transform into a world dominated by agriculturalists.

And this changed everything.

. . .

As the saying goes, no man is an island, and that is true for hunter-gatherers as well. During the Pleistocene, foraging groups were rarely organized into communities with an official or formal level of organization above the family. People could move as individuals or families; there were no official boundaries and no customs officials standing at the gate, checking visas.

This doesn't mean hunter-gatherers could go anywhere they wanted. Modern hunter-gatherers recognize boundaries, but instead of being hard and fast, the boundaries are permeable and negotiable. Once when walking through the forest in southwest Madagascar, my Mikea guide stopped suddenly and announced that we had just passed into Belo territory. I saw nothing to indicate a boundary, but my guide knew we were on land that "belonged" to others (people who lived in a hamlet called Belo).

But *belonged* is the wrong word. Nomadic hunter-gatherers don't see themselves as owning land (at least not until national governments forced the concept upon them) but as owning the right to be asked for permission to use a land's resources. Generally, among nomadic hunter-gatherers, that right is there for the asking. People don't trespass because they are sure to be discovered—either through the smoke from their fires or their tracks. Another time in Madagascar, my wife and I were resting in the shade of a hut after walking some twenty-five kilometers across the desert, when a stranger walked up and said to me, "You're the one with big feet." He had tracked my wife and me across the desert; our shoes had given us away as foreigners, and he wanted to know what we were doing (since foreigners often meant government officials—and trouble).

Hunter-gatherers almost always grant the right to use "their" land because in the near future the tables might be turned, and the host group will need the visitors to return the favor. But this changes once nomadic hunter-gatherers become sedentary. Recall that the process of becoming sedentary is like the game of musical chairs—everyone grabs a seat, a place on the landscape, and some of those places are better positioned than others, with better wild foods and better potential for agriculture. What happens during the inevitable bad years in these cases?

What happens is that those positioned on the poorer places will petition those in the better-endowed places for aid. But those in the well-endowed places will generally not need the assistance of those in poorer places because if a year is bad for the best places, it is probably horrible for the landscape's mediocre venues. On the other hand, if the well-endowed villagers deny the petitioners, they run the risk of retaliation because the potential cost of the violent overthrow of a village, death, doesn't seem too great to someone who might expect to starve anyway.

The hunting, gathering, and fishing societies of North America's Northwest Coast give us a clue as to what might have happened in these cases. These societies, such as the Kwakwaka'wakh (sometimes known as the Kwakiutl) held large feasts to mark a number of social occasions such as marriage and funerals. These feasts were known as *potlatches,* a word that comes from the coast's Chinook trade language and means "to give."[21] However, in Kwakwala, the word used is *pasa,* meaning "to flatten," as beneath a pile of gifts; that's an accurate definition, because potlatches were competitive feasts.

The point of the potlatch was to impress visitors with costumes, dances, magic tricks, and food, food, and more food. The height of the event was the giveaway, when the host, a high-ranking man, would make a very public display of giving away expensive things—blankets, canoes, slaves, and, the most expensive of all, painted and embossed "shields" of copper. Sometimes the host would simply destroy things—throw them in the sea, or toss them onto a bonfire. These feasts were no different from Gatsby-style parties of the rich and famous, what Thorstein Veblen, in 1899, famously called "conspicuous consumption."

The lead visitor at a potlatch was expected to reciprocate, and until he did so, he lost prestige in the eyes of both the host and the members of his own village. The reason has to do with how the host got all the stuff to give away. He did so by holding many small potlatches within his own village. He underwrote these small potlatches himself, and people had to reciprocate with a slightly greater amount of goods or lose prestige. It's similar to investment banking. When that ambitious man held a potlatch for another village, he was communicating to the guests just how many people stood with him. The more goods he had, the more power he possessed. The not-so-subtle message was "Look how much we can give away and it does us no harm. Don't even think about messing with us, because we can crush you. Now, let's be friends."[22]

Such feasts were probably an integral part of early village life in the Fertile Crescent. The need to produce food for those feasts might even have been a stimulus for agriculture, since more food makes for a more impressive feast. Some of the harvest, barley in particular, was used to make exclusively feast foods such as beer. (Some of the earliest intoxicating beverages we know of were brewed along the Yellow River in China, about 7000 B.C. Barley beer was brewed in modern-day Iran about 3400 B.C., and that was preceded by grape wine about 5400 B.C.) There was probably constant negotiation of status between villages, and feasts allowed them to judge each other's power. This created a new level of cooperation, albeit one tainted by underlying competition. The two often go hand in hand.

All of this—sedentary communities, agriculture, and competitive feasting—were brought on in large part by an imbalance in population and food. Agriculture solved that problem—and it might have created a new one.

. . .

I pointed out that hunter-gatherer populations in the past grew at very slow rates, about .04 percent per year. Compare that to current world-population growth of 1.14 percent (down from a maximum of 2.2 percent in the early 1960s).

Some researchers argue that this increase in growth rates began once hunter-gatherers became agriculturalists. Why that might be true is obvious: more food means more children. This is known as the Neolithic Demographic Transition. French demographer Jean-Pierre Bocquet-Appel argues that where archaeologists can find sufficiently large samples of hunter-gatherer burials, they find fewer burials of children and adolescents compared to those of adults than archaeologists find in the cemeteries of agriculturalists.[23] We might infer from this that most hunter-gatherer children survived to adulthood, and more kids in agricultural communities died. But ethnographic data show that 50 to 60 percent of children born in foraging societies fail to live to adulthood, and that sad fact seems to have continued well into the nineteenth century. So why aren't there more children and teenagers in the prehistoric hunter-gatherer cemeteries?

It's because hunter-gatherer women generally don't produce that many children. This is one reason why hunter-gatherer growth rates are so low and why it took so long for the world's population to reach one billion in the mid-nineteenth century. Anthropologists once thought that hunter-gatherers intentionally maintained their populations at low levels, even below carrying capacity, through herbal contraceptives, abortion, and postbirth sexual taboos. However, most herbal remedies or abortifacients don't actually work, and postbirth sexual taboos don't last as long as natural postbirth amenorrhea (the absence of menstruation), so they are ineffective even if practiced.

Hunter-gatherer women produce few offspring largely because of their workload and diet. A complex physiological process that involves the energy stored in a woman's body, how much a woman eats, and how much she works governs whether a woman can become pregnant. In brief, a woman who is thin, working hard, expending energy in breast-feeding, and not eating much—and this describes many hunter-gatherer women—will not ovulate regularly, or a fertilized egg might fail to implant in the uterus. A hunter-gatherer woman might give birth to four to six children during her reproductive years. If half of those die before reaching maturity, the result is a very, very slow growth rate and a nearly even balance between children and adults in cemeteries.

Agriculture changed this by changing the energetic demands on women. The availability of weaning foods (rice, potatoes, maize, and bread) meant that farming women could wean children at an earlier age, relaxing one pressure and allowing women to ovulate more quickly after birth.[24] Since hunter-gatherer women gather plant food, I'd imagine that early in the domestication process, women did most of the planting, tending, and harvesting. But, if ethnographic data on horticultural societies are any guide, men eventually turned their attention to the fields as well, as their time was better spent there than in the pursuit of game that was increasingly hard to find due to overhunting. So women's workload might have increased at first, but then it may have decreased and become more seasonally concentrated. A relaxation or seasonal concentration of workload would have altered women's physiology and also increased their ability to conceive. As a result, women in farming communities gave birth to more children during their reproductive years than women in hunting and gathering communities. Even with a continued mortality rate of 50–60 percent, an increase in fertility (e.g., from 4–6 to, say, 8–9 children per woman) would have increased the short-term growth rate. Short-term gains were probably held in check by periodic population crashes brought on by drought, frost, insect plagues, disease, or overuse of land. But even so, early farmers would sense population pressure and feel the need to make land more productive. And even if population was occasionally reduced, a slow positive rate of growth would exponentially increase the number of people living in the world.

Humans lived as nomadic hunter-gatherers for tens of thousands of years. But population growth eventually filled the world with people, made movement more difficult, and brought some groups to the carrying capacity of their local environments. Climate change and fortuitous plant genetics made agriculture a feasible option in some places, and hunter-gatherers seized it. Almost overnight in geologic time, hunter-gatherers became agriculturalists and created sedentary villages. Population continued to grow, and competition over living space increased. And once again, the past was nothing, *nothing* like what the future turned out to be.

CHAPTER 6

Kings and Chains

The Beginning of the State

The past always looks better than it was. It's only
pleasant because it isn't here.

—Finley Peter Dunne

If you ever find yourself in London with time to visit only one attraction,
I recommend the British Museum. Walk in through the front doors (it's
free) and enter the massive atrium. Straight ahead, in the atrium's center,
is the former library where Karl Marx wrote *Das Kapital*. Walk around
the library to the left and through a deceptively unassuming door. There
in front of you will be the Rosetta stone, one of the world's most significant archaeological finds, an emblem of the fourth beginning.

I wish I could say that an archaeologist discovered the Rosetta stone
through careful research and dogged fieldwork. But no; it was found in
Egypt in 1799 by Pierre-François Bouchard, a member of Napoleon's
military force, while rebuilding the Ottoman Turks' fortifications. Fortunately, Bouchard thought the stone might have historical value and he
set it aside for study by French scholars. But the British defeated the
French forces in 1801, so today the stone rests in the British Museum
rather than in the Louvre.

Discovery of the Rosetta stone was just the beginning of what archaeologist Brian Fagan called the rape of the Nile.[1] By the mid-nineteenth
century, Egypt's archaeology, as well as that of Greece, Italy, and the
Near East, was for sale to anyone daring enough to move humongous
blocks of stone. The Nile received particular attention because its
archaeology was, and is, stunning—the pyramids, tombs, statuary, palaces, and towering columns. The dirty laundry of many famous muse-
ums is that they got some of their best stuff by pillaging conquered

nations or by buying it at bargain-basement prices from cash-starved rulers.[2] In the spirit of full disclosure, I'll point out that these plunderers created the field of archaeology. To be polite, we call them antiquarians and we treat them the way everyone treats their eccentric uncle: we don't like to talk about them.

Sitting on your perch in space, watching the history of the world unfold, you might feel some fanny fatigue at this point. But you soon forget any discomfort, because after agriculture appears, change comes fast and furious. The last ten thousand years, and especially the last five thousand years, witness more change than the previous six million. This is the time of cities, swords and spears, gold and silver, temples and palaces, roads, bridges, jewelry, spices, chariots, money—and men and women in chains. This is the time of states.

For anthropologists the term *state* refers to societies that have at least three levels of political hierarchy: most simply, a ruling class, a bureaucratic class, and laborers. More important, these levels entail relationships quite different from those of the foraging and horticultural societies that dominated the world for tens of thousands of years. Only a few people were buried in a pyramid that took forty years and thousands of backs to build. In fact, a select few benefitted far more than the masses from developments in trade, the arts, and the sciences. A few were rulers, but most were ruled. Paleolithic hunter-gatherers would have been shocked.

. . .

What is most noticeable from your perch in space is that the many small, sleepy agricultural communities scattered around the world of ten thousand to five thousand years ago have been replaced by large cities with massive public architecture. In addition to houses are buildings that provide a specific function—as places of worship, burial, business, or bureaucracy—but the purpose of others, says anthropologist Paul Roscoe, is to leave visitors, as well as the rank and file, in "shock and awe."[3] In a way, public architecture is an expansion of the competitive feasts of the early agricultural era. They tell visitors just who they are dealing with. And there is no better example of shock and awe than Egypt in the days of the pharaohs.

When you visit Egypt's pyramids on the Giza plateau, just outside Cairo, stand at the base of Khufu's pyramid and look up. You won't be able to see the top. But all three pyramids there are impressive, along with the Sphinx and numerous ancillary temples. Built between 2550 and 2475 B.C., Giza's pyramids were originally covered with polished limestone (scavenged by later builders), which would have made them shine brilliant white and be visible for miles. Their simple lines make them visually stunning, but they are not simple structures. Their architects understood the complex ways that massive piles of rock behave. For example, the central burial chamber in Khufu's pyramid has several cantilevered roofs to direct the vectors of force away from the tomb so it would not be crushed. There are false tombs (to misdirect grave robbers, but these usually didn't work so well) and narrow slits built through many, many meters of rock (which probably had a symbolic rather than functional significance).

You might have heard some nonsense about how aliens from outer space built these remarkable structures. Proponents of this idea claim that it must have been aliens because there's no evidence of Egyptians learning the craft and no way to move two- to three-ton stones with ancient technology. These claims are false. Egyptians learned to build these magnificent structures the old-fashioned way: through trial and error.

Long before they built pyramids, Egyptians buried their dead in mastabas—low, square structures of cut stone, with burial chambers carved into the bedrock below. The first pyramid, built by the Pharaoh Djoser at Saqqara about 2620 B.C., south of Cairo, was not a true pyramid but a stepped pyramid, a set of increasingly smaller mastabas stacked on top of one another. Later, architects of the Pharaoh Sneferu tried their hand at a true pyramid.

Initially, the architects built a small pyramid at an angle of 60 degrees, but the structure sat on unstable sands and subsided. The architects increased its size and reduced the pyramid's exterior slope to 55 degrees. They laid the massive building blocks so that they sloped inward (a technique borrowed from mastaba construction), but this eventually made the structure unstable, so about halfway up, the builders began laying the stones flat and reduced the exterior angle to 44 degrees. This tactic gave the pyramid its name: the Bent Pyramid. Unfortunately, problems continued, caused by poorly laid blocks, low-quality clay mortar, and a sandy foundation. Sneferu finally abandoned this pyramid and built another nearby, the Red Pyramid, as his final resting place. This pyramid suffered no problems, and by the time Sneferu's son, Khufu, began his massive building project at Giza about 2550 B.C., Egyptian architects had honed their craft.[4]

That included learning how to move massive blocks of stone. Experiments show that with enough ropes and manpower, as depicted in tomb paintings, just about anything can be moved. (The Europeans who pillaged Egyptian sites in the nineteenth century used similar technology.) Egyptians built ramps at a low angle; set planed, greased planks at right angles to the ramps' edges; and filled the interstices with slippery gypsum. With such ramps, many strong backs can pull large rocks to dizzying heights. Remote sensing studies of the Giza pyramids suggest the builders may have moved stone up such ramps in tunnels that spiraled around the circumference of the pyramids. The builders then filled those tunnels from the top down.

People dragged large rocks around the landscape long before the time of Egypt's pharaohs. The site of Göbekli Tepe in Turkey consists of some twenty circular structures of T-shaped pillars, each weighing up to twenty tons and decorated with bas-relief bulls, foxes, and cranes. The earliest of these structures was built about 9000 B.C. (during agriculture's early beginnings). And there is Stonehenge in the United Kingdom, first built about 3000 B.C. Its sarsen stones, weighing up to forty tons each, were collected locally, but smaller bluestones, a mere one or two tons each, were moved from an outcrop some 220 kilometers distant. There were actually quite a few of these henges built throughout Britain (some of which were massive woodhenges).

What is different about Stonehenge and Göbekli Tepe is that they are not embedded in a community but sit by themselves. This changes once the state appears, and many ceremonial structures—temples, oracles, amphitheaters, schools, and political structures like the Roman Senate—are embedded within communities, where access to them was both figuratively and literally controlled. Early religious structures strike me as more inclusive, designed to unify; the state's religious and political structures appear more exclusive, intended to control and communicate who belonged and who did not.

These massive public projects appear in places where agriculture is especially responsive to efforts to increase production. This includes irrigation in dry lands and terracing on hillsides to create more flat land in mountainous country. The Aztecs, whose capital sat in the middle of a vast wetland, built *chinampas,* long, linear islands of rich, fertile muck dredged by hand from the wetland's bottom. The Aztecs kept their fields fertile by collecting human waste and dumping it on their fields. These efforts raised their region's carrying capacity and allowed the population to continue to grow. (Modern agriculture continues to increase production with, for example, rotary irrigation fields, commercial fertilizers, fish farms, and genetically modified foods.)

Increased production wasn't simply to support a growing population but also to free some people from food production. This included a state's elite and bureaucrats, but increased production was really necessary to free up laborers for a state's shock-and-awe feats. People building pyramids (often for decades) are people not working fields. Those laborers had to be supported, which means agriculture had to become more productive. Thus the need for irrigation in dry areas, terracing in mountainous ones, and so on. The key ingredients for agriculture are soil, water, and sunlight, so it's not surprising that the agricultural intensification integral to the formation of states often appeared along rivers, with their rich alluvial plains, and in sunny, desert areas where warm-climate grasses had been domesticated.

One of these centers lay along the southern Tigris and Euphrates Rivers, in modern-day Iraq, where irrigation agriculture began about 6000 B.C. The Uruk state formed about 4000 B.C., and it boasted the world's first city, Uruk (known in the Bible as Erech). After Uruk, states appeared in other places (see figure 3). Egypt's first state shows up soon after 3000 B.C., and the Minoan civilization on the island of Crete appears about 2100 B.C. The Greek civilization of Mycenae appears by 1600 B.C., with city-states appearing later, about 1000 B.C. In China, public architecture appears about 2000 B.C., and along the Indus Valley in Pakistan by 2600 B.C. Similar ceremonial centers are at Angkor Wat in Cambodia and at Great Zimbabwe in Zimbabwe (the country acquired its name from the archaeological site). Cities such as Uruk were crucial to some early states, while other states developed ceremonial centers surrounded by smaller settlements that provided labor. Eventually, though, cities would become central to the political and trade functions of the state. In many cases, they were walled as a principal line of defense (visit Xi'an in China to see a wonderfully preserved example).

States appeared a bit later in the New World, perhaps held back by the lack of domesticated animals that could provide meat and milk and that could pull plows to increase agricultural production. Nonetheless, the New World eventually also saw large civic and ceremonial centers. Shortly after A.D. 1000, people built impressive flat-topped earthen pyramids at places such as Cahokia, Illinois, and Moundville, Alabama. About the same time, people in the southwest United States built multistoried pueblos with hundreds of rooms in Chaco Canyon and connected them to the world beyond the canyon through wide roads.

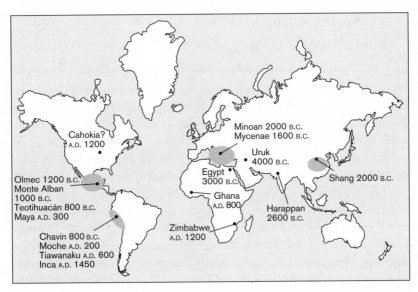

FIGURE 3. Where and when the world's early states first appeared. Whether some of these reached true state status is debated.

Archaeologists do not consider these cases to be "states," but they are examples of the growing complexity of social and political life that followed on the heels of agriculture.

In Mexico, Olmec ceremonial centers appeared along the Gulf coast about 1200 B.C. and were followed by a succession of other centers: Monte Alban with its hilltop palace, and Teotihuacán, an eight-square-mile center of flat-topped temples, the arrow-straight Avenue of the Dead, thousands of residences, and the New World's largest stone structure, the Pyramid of the Sun. By the time the Spanish arrived in A.D. 1519, the action had shifted south, to the Aztecs' capital, Tenochtitlán, situated on an island in a lake (drained long ago; Mexico City now occupies the lakebed). To the south, the Maya built temples and palaces in the Central American jungle, in the dry Yucatan Peninsula, and in the highlands of southern Mexico, reaching an apogee between 250 B.C. and A.D. 900.

In the Andes Mountains and along the bone-dry Peruvian coast, a succession of complex social forms appears beginning about 1500 B.C. The last of these was the Inca empire, whose rulers built palaces where modern-day Cuzco sits, and at places such as Machu Picchu, where elite homes were balanced on a knife-edge ridge high above the Rio Uru-bamba.[5]

. . .

From your perch in space, you witness a rapid development of the sciences and arts once states are born. You see grand architecture (such as the Romans' arched aqueducts and the flying buttresses of Europe's medieval cathedrals), and threshing mills powered by draft animals or waterwheels. You see the field of mathematics appear, to assist with architectural calculations, astronomical observations, and records of trade. Copper tools appeared in the late Neolithic, about 5000 B.C., in southern Europe, Turkey, and northern Iran. Bronze (copper with a bit of tin added) appeared later, about 3300 B.C., spread rapidly through Europe between 2500 and 1500 B.C., and was quickly followed by iron smelting after 1000 B.C.[6] Gold and silver working appear somewhat later; those metals are too soft for any sort of serious functional tools, but that property is what allowed them to become fine jewelry, emblems of status and prestige. The wheel appears in the Old World by 3500 B.C. (in central Europe), and spreads rapidly; it's in China by 1400 B.C. (Save for some children's toys, the wheel never appears in the precontact New World, most likely because of the lack of draft animals to pull carts and chariots. However, this did not stop New World peoples from constructing their own architectural marvels, such as the Maya pyramids.)

In both the Old and New Worlds, rulers supported court artisans who provided entertainment and demonstrated the ruler's power. The state co-opted the abilities of the supersymbolers and began the rapid technological development of music, the arts, and science that would result in Beethoven's symphonies, the Sistine Chapel, Maya astronomy, and China's Forbidden City.

Trade became as extensive as transportation technology permitted and professional traders dared. In the Old World, intrepid traders opened the 6,400-kilometer Silk Road by 200 B.C. A series of routes, the Silk Road would eventually connect China with medieval Europe and provide European elites with goods used to signal their status: silk, spices, precious stones, and jewelry. New World trade was more limited, but still extensive. For example, copper bells, skeletons of macaws, turquoise, obsidian, and remnants of chocolate in ceramic containers found in pueblos of the American Southwest point to trade with Mexico and Central America.

Trade itself was not new; in fact, it had existed for millennia, but as an informal system of barter, or "gifts" whose purpose was largely social rather than economic. That system worked fine between people who knew each other and who expected to see one another repeatedly. With a growing population, however, traders needed to exchange goods with distant partners whom they might not see again, and in situations where the goods to be exchanged could not be present at the same time and place. This made barter difficult. Formal money solved this problem (the earliest coins come from Lydia, in Turkey, and date to the seventh century B.C.) and required some cooperative understanding (we agree that this round bit of silver bearing a particular design represents X baskets of wheat or its equivalent). This continues today with modern currencies and their international valuation.

Writing systems also developed in state societies. In the Old World there were Egypt's hieroglyphics (3000 B.C.), the Near East's cuneiform (3100 B.C.), Pakistan's Indus Valley script (2500 B.C.), and Chinese character writing (1500 B.C.). Later, there was Phoenician (1000 B.C.), Linear A (1600 B.C.), Linear B (1450 B.C.), and the Greek alphabet (750 B.C.). In the New World, Maya, Zapotec, and Mixtec hieroglyphs appeared by 300 B.C. In some cases (e.g., Egyptian and Maya hieroglyphs), written records were part of the shock-and-awe tactics of public architecture, used to extol a leader's virtues and successes, and to remind everyone why the king was king. Cuneiform writing, on the other hand, was used to record mundane business transactions and tax payments (on thousands and thousands of clay tablets). These reflected the need to keep formal records between distant entrepreneurs or state tax collectors, records that maintained honesty with strangers and especially adversaries. In China, some of the earliest writing appears on turtle shells and cattle scapulae as well as on bronze ritual vessels about 1300 B.C. during the Shang state; some of these were used for prophecy, but such divination was linked to decisions made by the ruling class.

All of this material culture—counting systems, writing, the sciences, and the arts—is what many people call "civilization." And it is remarkable. Walk among the Maya ruins of Palenque or the temples at Egypt's Luxor and, like archaeologists, you can't help but wish to go back in time and see these places in action. And yet, you might regret it if you could. Because all the architecture, art, music, math, and writing, all the spices and silk and chocolate and Greek statues and Doric columns tell of a change in the way people understood and treated one another. And it wasn't always pleasant.

. . .

In agricultural and foraging societies, even the large, socially complex ones that anthropologists call chiefdoms, kinship is the dominant principle that links people. In ancient Hawai'i, a society that at the time of European contact was a huge chiefdom, the ruling chief still referred to people below him as his "children." In such societies, kinship provides the primary "rules" that guide how people behave toward one another. Anthropologists who work with foraging and horticultural societies are often "adopted" into the society, normally by a prominent family. Because without that kinship link, the anthropologists is . . . who? People in the community wonder: Can we trust this stranger? Can we joke with him or her? Should we be deferential? Can we talk about private things? The answers to those questions are resolved once they know a person's kin relation. If a man adopts, say, a male anthropologist as his "son," then everyone knows that whatever their particular kin relationship is to that man's biological son is now the relationship they have with the anthropologist. Everyone can stop wondering now.

But in state societies, the kin linkage between the rulers and the ruled is severed. Don't misunderstand: kinship still matters enormously in state societies. Everyone in the United Kingdom knows at least the next four or five people in line for the throne after Queen Elizabeth.[7] In the United States, we believe that kin connections shouldn't matter, yet the genealogies of presidents, senators, and representatives tell us that it does. However, in state societies, kinship matters more *within* than *between* classes. In early state societies, a new set of relationships was added, ones that entailed codified relations with the ruling body, such as government officials, tax collectors, and military commanders. Relations with these people are governed by cultural and legal rules. You don't have to know police or tax collectors personally in order to know how to behave in their presence. The same happens when we have classes. British citizens don't have to know someone personally in order to know to whom one should bow or curtsey or whom to address as Sir, Madam, My Lord, or Your Royal Highness.

The shift away from kinship as a guiding principle was crucial to states, and it played a role in two important changes: dramatic social inequality and organized war. These two new elements of life underwrote the remarkable achievements of early civilizations. It's much easier to enslave people and get them to build pyramids or to send them onto the battlefield as cannon fodder if they are not your relatives and, in fact, if you don't consider them to be as human as you are. Two of the great problems of our era, inequality and war, began five thousand years ago. How did this happen?

. . .

When my pessimistic Kentucky student from chapter 1 claimed that "this is the way things always have been and this is the way things always will be," he was probably thinking about war. Haven't we always beaten each other up? Isn't war just the extension of one *Homo erectus* whacking another with a handy rock? In a word, no.

Visit Istanbul's archaeology museum and you can see the world's first known peace treaty (a copy is on display in the United Nations building). It was signed between the Egyptians and the Hittites (an empire located in today's Turkey) in 1258 B.C., some fifteen years after the Battle of Kadesh ended in a stalemate. Deciding, finally, that neither could defeat the other, Ramesses II and Hattusili III decided to cooperate. Before their gods, they pledged to return runaways to each other's control (Hattusili III had defeated his nephew, Mursili II, for the Hittite throne, and Mursili had fled to Egypt, where Ramesses protected him). And each pledged to come to the other's aid if attacked. The treaty is almost sweet, like two lovers who decide to kiss and make up.

Until you recall that the Battle of Kadesh involved horrific slaughter and enormous expense. Both sides fielded thousands of soldiers and had invested many resources in the technology of war and full-time armies. Ramesses had even built a new capital in the Nile delta in order to manufacture weaponry. (Ramesses needed his new alliance because he was also fighting Libyan tribal peoples along his empire's western edge.)

This level of fighting makes you sit forward on your perch in space. Violence is not new; people have whacked each other for millennia. But now, with the appearance of the state, we see weapons designed *specifically to kill people:* swords, spears, and pikes, and eventually longbows, crossbows, and the whole wicked menagerie of medieval warfare. As a response, people also invested in defensive works such as palisaded villages, walled towns, and castles with tall keeps designed for a final stand.

Many ancient states become insatiable empires. In the Near East the Hittite Empire (1450–1220 B.C.) was followed by that of the Assyrians and then by the Achaemenid Persian Empire, brought to an end by

Alexander the Great in 334 B.C. Along the Mediterranean, various powers rose and fell beginning about 2000 B.C.: Minoans, Myceneans, Phoenicians, Etruscans, the Greeks, and the Romans. And we could go on into the medieval history of Europe, the Ottoman Empire (A.D. 1299–1922), and the colonial powers of the Dutch, Portuguese, Spanish, French and British. Insatiable leaders such as Genghis Khan are followed by Napoleon, Hitler, Stalin, Mao Zedong, and Pol Pot.

In China walled villages appear about 2500 B.C. during the Longshan culture and thereafter began a long succession of dynasties: Xia, Shang, Zhou, and Qin, whose first ruler, Qin Shi Huangdi, began construction of the Great Wall, made the writing system uniform, and created a hierarchical governing system. The Qin dynasty was followed by the Han dynasty, which was followed by a series of kingdoms, some encompassing just portions of modern-day China and by the Jin, Sui, and Song dynasties. By A.D. 1271, the Mongols, under Kublai Khan, ruled China and established the Yuan dynasty, which was followed by the Ming dynasty, the Qing dynasty, the first republic of China (A.D. 1912–1949), and then Mao's People's Republic of China. Of course, a great deal happens throughout this five-thousand-year period; I don't wish to shortchange China's or any other culture's history. But from an archaeological perspective, the main threads of the story don't change: It's a five-thousand-year contest for power and control. And the same story plays out in Europe, Mexico, the Central Andes, Africa, and Southeast and Central Asia.

It just so happens that recorded history appears during the era of states due to the writing systems needed to proclaim victories, to record taxes, and to write laws. If it seems that history is just one damn war after another, it's because, once states appear, that's how it was. It's understandable why anyone who knows history would think the future is bleak.

A century ago the world fought the First World War, known at the time as the Great War and, by the time it was over, as the "war to end all wars." Sadly, it didn't turn out that way. You would be justified in thinking that war is here to stay. We fight, you might think, because it's who we are. There is no denying the fact that violence has served us in the competitive process of evolution. It is part of our behavioral repertoire. Does that mean that war is inevitable, that it will always dominate what Lincoln called the "better angels of our nature"?

. . .

Although this chapter is about state societies, I'm going to turn to hunter-gatherers to answer this question about war because many people imagine hunter-gatherers are closer to human nature. They think that if they could go back to when all people lived as hunter-gatherers, when life was (they suppose) less cluttered and complicated, they would see human nature in the raw.

Let me be clear on this: hunter-gatherers, ancient or modern, do not reflect human nature any more than do other categories of people. But since many people *think* hunter-gatherers display human nature in the raw, let's see what foragers have to say about a human propensity for violence.

Western ideas about human nature fall into one of two camps. The patron saint of one is Thomas Hobbes, and of the other, Jean-Jacques Rousseau. In 1651, Hobbes famously described life before society in *Leviathan:* "No Arts; no Letters, no Society, and which is worst of all, continuall feare, and danger of violent death; And the life of man, solitary, poor, nasty, brutish, and short." But a century later, Rousseau wrote in his *Discourse on the Origin and Basis of Inequality among Men* that "nothing is more gentle than man in his primitive state." So, which is it? Are hunter-gatherers the original hippies or the ultimate road warriors?

The first thing you should know is that hunter-gatherers don't live lives of perfect bliss, but they do have low rates of *nonlethal* aggression, such as fistfights. This isn't because they're "nice people" but because of the cultural denial of aggression in small, egalitarian communities. When the anthropologist Jean Briggs entitled her 1970 book on an Inuit family *Never in Anger,* she didn't mean that the Inuit are never ticked off, only that it's inappropriate to show anger.[8] But in small communities, you will inevitably tread on other people's toes, and pent-up tensions can erupt unexpectedly. The resulting violence often has no objective other than to express anger. Sometimes that anger turns into violence and someone may die, but as a result of insane rage, not calculated risk.

Warfare is different because it *is* calculated risk. Borrowing anthropologist Douglas Fry's definition, warfare is "relatively impersonal lethal aggression between communities."[9] *Impersonal* doesn't mean that warriors aren't passionate. In fact, leaders must inspire passion if they want followers to put their lives on the line and kill someone. They have to make it personal. War is nasty business, and while its superficial goal is revenge or retaliation, for a *group* to be compelled to fight, the goal must also be to secure some advantage such as slaves, women, food, territory, or security through a preemptive strike.

Sometimes the source of conflicts can sound silly, so silly that it reinforces the stereotype that men will fight over anything. For example, in

1860, on North America's Northwest Coast, the Yakutat Tlingit attacked the Sitka Tlingit during a potlatch because the Sitka had out-sung the Yakutat two years in a row.[10] That's right, a fight over a DJ's playlist. But those songs are a mere index for a far more significant fact. To retaliate after the first embarrassment, the Yakutat learned songs from a neighboring group. But unknown to the Yakutat, the Sitka also increased their repertoire with songs from the Aleut. The songs themselves didn't matter; what mattered was that they were an index of allies. With their more extensive repertoire, the Sitka proclaimed themselves, once again, more powerful than the Yakutat. The Yakutat had to strike preemptively or risk being perceived as weak and vulnerable.

Violence is one option that humans can use to achieve an objective. But like all options, it comes with a cost, and that cost could be steep. You could lose what you have, get hurt, or die. And even when it's successful, violence is costly since it makes enemies and drains resources from other needs. Organized violence solves one immediate problem but it creates other, longer-term ones. We all know this, and yet at times humans clearly judge the cost of war as worth the benefit. Why?

Let's first consider what starts war among hunter-gatherers, because what starts war can differ from what continues war. We might assume that wars start when a village feels its crucial resources, such as food, shelter, or mates, are threatened. Food is perhaps most crucial because it's the most immediate. When things go bad in a hunter-gatherer's neighborhood—a drought, range fire, illness, whatever—they usually follow Ronald Reagan's advice and vote with their feet. They pack up and move.

This is an easy solution, but not if there's someone already living where you want to live *and* if they too are already under pressure. This means that we might expect warfare and violence to become more common as population pressure increases. In analyzing hunter-gatherer ethnographic data, that is exactly what I've found. As population pressure increases so too does the incidence of warfare as well as the incidence of homicide.[11] When there are many people relative to the food base, hunter-gatherers fight. And there's nothing remarkable in that. Violence might not be human nature, but wanting to survive is. Put anyone between a rock and a hard place and they'll fight—whether they're hunter-gatherers or university faculty.

Archaeological data seem to carry the same message. I say "seem to" because trying to study prehistoric human violence requires human skeletal remains, where violence is recorded as parry wounds on the bones of the forearms, as stone points embedded in bone and body cavities, and as depression fractures on skulls.[12] Unfortunately, skeletal remains don't always preserve well and they become scarce as we go further back in time.

Nonetheless, most archaeologists would say that the earliest evidence of warfare comes from the 11,000 B.C. site of Jebel Sahaba, in northern Sudan. That evidence is pretty clear. Twenty-four people have multiple stone projectile points in their body cavities. They were "pin-cushioned," and some have points embedded in their neck vertebrae suggesting they were executed. This is war, or something close to it.

But Jebel Sahaba stands out precisely because it's a rare case.[13] Archaeologists Jonathan Haas and Mathew Piscitelli studied nearly three thousand burials dating to more than 12,000 years old, and they could find only four more cases of warfare-like violence.[14] Likewise, anthropologist Brian Ferguson found little evidence of violence in prehistoric Europe until after the appearance of agriculture and, in fact, after the appearance of state societies.[15]

In North America, archaeological research shows that warfare occurred primarily at a time when population density was high and when carrying capacity declined. In fact, evidence of warfare spikes in several areas, such as the Great Plains, southern California, and the Southwest during a climatic period known as the Medieval Warm Period, about A.D. 950–1250.[16] North America's aboriginal population had reached a peak, probably its greatest peak, about A.D. 1000. Then the hot, dry Medieval Warm Period pulled the rug out from under everyone, diminishing carrying capacity and increasing violence as people scrambled to control key locations.

The result appears in places such as Crow Creek, a horticultural village in South Dakota where nearly five hundred people, most of the village's inhabitants, were massacred in A.D. 1325. In the Southwest, in places such as Mesa Verde, maize farmers moved into difficult-to-reach cliff dwellings between A.D. 1190 and 1300. They perched their granaries on the sides of cliffs, accessible only by rope. In nearby regions, villagers moved to the tops of equally inaccessible buttes. Many sites of this time period contain human skeletons that bear the marks of violent death and even of cannibalism.

Ancient hunter-gatherers and early farmers whacked one another every now and again (recall our discussion of Ötzi in chapter 2), but war is a cultural, not a natural, behavior. Nomadic foragers value alliances and social connections because they cope with problems by moving in with neighbors and, quid pro quo, by allowing neighbors to move in with them. They did this because the nomadic life forces interdependence. This doesn't mean that hunter-gatherers hugged each other and sang "Kumbaya" whenever they met. In fact, when one group of nomadic Australian Aborigines sought refuge in the land of another, the initial meeting was often tense and involved displays of strength. They were suspicious of one another, and yet their culture was such that both sides could see, albeit begrudgingly, the value of cooperation. They were what they had to be.

And what people had to be changed as they switched from life in nomadic camps to that in sedentary villages. The material conditions of life tipped the fundamental strategy away from one type of cooperation toward another, one of vigilance and alliances to create strength against another, as Ramesses II and Hattusili III did. Sedentary villagers need to be prepared to implement a violent option, and that fact changes their culture. People come to value belligerence, to use generosity as a club, and to compete for prestige through violence.

This set of traits is more prevalent among sedentary hunter-gatherers than among nomadic ones. Here's what a nomadic Ju/'hoan man of southern Africa said to anthropologist Richard Lee: "When a young man kills much meat, he comes to think of himself as a chief. . . . We refuse one who boasts, for someday his pride will make him kill somebody. So we always speak of his meat as worthless. In this way we cool his heart and make him gentle." In contrast, here is what one Kwakwaka'wakh man said to his fellow coastal villagers: "You know that every time when the tribes come to our village [for a potlatch], we always have four or five more to give blankets away than they have. Therefore, take care, young chiefs! else you will lose your high and lofty name; for our grandfathers were never beaten in war of blood nor in war of wealth, and therefore all the tribes are below us Kwakiutl in rank."[17]

Warfare is linked to the material conditions of life. Those conditions can create a culture of violence, one that worships and rewards success in battle, one that elevates male warriors over women. This culture of violence can be insidious and hard to overcome, but it does not simply reflect human nature.

. . .

Cross-cultural studies of many kinds of human populations, not just hunter-gatherers, shed more light on war. Decades ago, anthropologists began to compile data from all ethnographic studies into the Human

Relations Area Files, or HRAF, housed at Yale University.[18] Anthropologists Carol Ember and the late Melvin Ember used these data to conduct cross-cultural studies of warfare. They found a statistically significant correlation between *unpredictable* events, such as food shortfalls, and warfare.[19] Societies put mechanisms into place to cope with regular, anticipated problems, such as seasonal shortfalls, but unpredictable events can push people over the edge. An extraordinarily severe winter or dry summer can affect such a large area that you end up with neighbors who can't help you, or whom you can't help because your own surplus is too meager. Rising population density only makes such events more likely because a shortage of food or water at a density of ten people per square kilometer is not as bad as the same shortage at one hundred people per square kilometer.

The Embers found that the pattern held true for all societies except states. State societies need large fighting forces, often standing armies. If the harvest has been lost (due to drought or locusts, for example), then they might be unable to field a force sufficient to conquer or rob a neighbor. In addition, state societies *are* states because they've conquered some neighbors *so that* they are able to redistribute resources from one area to another. Many ancient states became empires, expanding outward and conquering many smaller political units; these then provided resources and/or labor to the capital. Because of this wider resource base, states might be more immune to unpredictable events.

This doesn't mean states are free of violence—in fact, quite the contrary. Nonstate societies might conduct small-scale raids or kill one person in retaliation for a death of their own, but Carol Ember found that states are far more likely to participate in atrocities. In fact, they excel at scaring the hell out of their neighbors by murdering noncombatants, torturing captives, raping women, public mutilation and execution, the taking of trophies (e.g., heads), and the destruction of sacred property (e.g., statues and temples). And these tactics are taken not just against neighbors but against folks within the state as well. Every Machiavellian ruler knows that subjects have to be kept in line, and a few hangings, beheadings, or heads impaled on spears can go a long way toward doing so. Dictators must be ruthless because they have only two options: remain in control at the top or, like Libya's Mu'ammar al-Gadhafi, meet an ignoble end in a drainage ditch.

States also glorify the horrific side of warfare. In a nonstate society, you earn points by getting the other side to back down or by embarrassing your opponent. A Lakota man scored by counting *coup*, touching an enemy without killing him (which says, "I can come close enough to touch you, but I am fast and clever enough to get away. I'm better than you. Don't mess with me"). In states, you gain glory by making war hurt badly. And by glorifying warfare, states promote a culture of violence that ensures a continuation of warfare. I'm reminded of an elderly German man I met on the island of Yap in the western Pacific. He was a quiet, polite and intellectual man, traveling the world to grieve the death of his wife. Sitting on a sunny beach he admitted to me that he had fought under Hitler, and that when he was seventeen, his greatest fear was that the war would end before he had his chance to fight. He hung his head, ashamed and embarrassed, unable to believe his own youthful naiveté.

The origin of states begins a vicious cultural cycle. States become empires and exploit their resident populations mercilessly, as leaders "buy off" their potential competitors and create allies within their ranks. The result is waves of destruction across the landscape. Sitting on your perch in space, you avert your eyes.

. . .

Culture, our constructed vision of the world, has such a powerful pull that many leaders fool themselves, and their followers, into thinking that they are fighting for "sacred values," the term that Thomas Jefferson used to describe the Declaration of Independence, when they are actually doing it for material gain or to leverage political advantage over a rival.

Someone gains from war, certainly the leaders, who in ancient times acquired possessions, territory, taxes, and slaves. In large state societies, many members benefit from war in terms of employment and security. But others are convinced or coerced into participating; they pay the price. Usually, they are the powerless. Vietnam was known as a poor man's war, but the same was true of the First World War.[20]

Today's most dramatic example is that of Islamist suicide bombers. Anthropologist Scott Atran has studied radical Islamist insurgency movements and has interviewed jihadists and the families of suicide bombers.[21] Contrary to what many in the Western world believe, male suicide bombers aren't motivated by the promise of a boatload of virgins in heaven. Most don't even believe that. Instead, they are motivated by values that anyone can agree with: brotherhood, loyalty, adventure, and dreams of a better world. Since they kill innocent people, the Western world vilifies suicide bombers. Yet in the 1960s, Americans who could not even identify Vietnam on a map went there to fight for "freedom," without much knowledge of the Cold War era's "domino theory." Many, I expect, went for the same reasons that jihadis blow themselves up: they didn't want to lose face in front of their friends and family. I was too young to have served in Vietnam, but old enough to think about it, and had I been drafted, the only reason I would have gone would have been to please my father.

That some people bear the cost of war while others reap the benefits points to a crucial element of the culture of states, one that evolution never saw coming when selection created a cultural animal out of Pleistocene hominins.

. . .

When I was a graduate student at the University of Michigan in the early 1980s, the Museum of Anthropology would hold an annual event for students and staff known as the Ugly Artifact Contest. Students would search the museum's collections for the oddest, funniest, or ugliest artifacts they could find. An entry one year was a collection of ceramic bowls, what are known as "beveled-rim" bowls. These are found by the thousands in Uruk-period sites in southern Iraq and are as much as 5,700 years old. They were mass-produced, fashioned on molds through a process that would have made Henry Ford jealous. Archaeologists Joyce Marcus and Kent Flannery call them the prehistoric equivalent of Styrofoam cups.[22]

Interestingly, they come in three sizes, 0.9 liters, 0.65 liters, and 0.45 liters, or a full serving, two-thirds of a serving, and a half serving. These are ration bowls. We don't know what they held (barley gruel is a good guess), but they point to someone being compensated for something. And that something was probably labor because it took vast amounts to make the temples, palaces, marketplaces, and roads that appeared with the Uruk state. The people who built those places did not get to use them. They were not carried in litters. They did not enjoy the fruits of a court's artisans, wear jewelry, or have clothes fashioned from exotic materials. Civilization's dirty secret is that it was built on the backs of slaves, indentured servants, and peasants. We see poverty for the first time in state societies.

Exactly how inequality arises is puzzling. If you could go back in time to when everyone lived as hunter-gatherers, you might think that everyone was poverty-stricken. And yet, when everyone in the world is just like you, has just as many beads, and carries all their belongings in a simple net bag, then no one is poor. Inequality matters when some have what others don't and can't have, when some believe that they have the legitimate right to put other humans in chains, or to subjugate women.

Nomadic hunter-gatherers and many small-scale agricultural communities have social orders that anthropologists label "egalitarian." This doesn't mean that everyone is equal. Hunter-gatherers know that people are not equal. Some folks are better hunters, some are better at crafting arrow points or baskets, some are healers and know the medicinal uses of plants. What *egalitarian* means is that *everyone has equal access to the critical resources of life:* food, water, mates, living space, and the technology to acquire these. The only variable is individual talent and effort, and the power that such differences might bestow is kept in check by peer pressure.

Egalitarian communities make sure that no one thinks himself or herself superior, even those who truly do have superior abilities. People need to be reminded of this because all of us can be selfish from time to time. We can't help it. Evolution has designed us to look out for number one. But at the same time, we realize that we need others. No matter how good we are, at some point we need help, and we might have to be reminded of that periodically (recall our discussion of sharing in chapter 4). Foraging camps are endless gossip sessions of who did what to whom, who owes who, and who is acting like a jerk. Evolution has designed us to pay attention to such gossip because doing so is in our best interest.

Gossip usually revolves around cultural values, values that people have internalized as "natural." When a Bushman brings a fat antelope into camp, he will apologize for not being able to find anything better, although he knows it's a good kill. By publicly berating himself, he is saying, "I know this is a good kill. I know I'm contributing more than others, but I'm not going to hold that against anyone." This is the culture of nomadic hunter-gatherers. It's a culture where those with superior abilities are not allowed to exert control over others, to restrict others' access to the basic needs of life. And, in fact, it's a culture where those with superior abilities might want to exert that control but would feel soiled if they did so.

This changes somewhat with agriculture, but it's not agriculture itself that causes the change—it's not that maize or wheat turns people into selfish braggarts and petty captains. Instead, I think that sedentary village life is the culprit.

. . .

We might think that any nomadic forager would jump at the chance to live in a sedentary village, to enjoy the benefits of a substantial house and more material possessions. We might think that hunter-gatherers would quickly find a favored spot on the landscape, one near a stand of wild wheat or the mouth of a salmon stream, and settle down.

But sedentary villages appear rarely among prehistoric hunter-gatherers, and when they do, they appear late in any region's prehistoric cultural sequence. Why become sedentary? As we saw in the last chapter, it happens when the cost of moving is high relative to the benefit. This fact sets into motion a process with important social implications.

If you can't move, you have to expand your diet, taking lower-return-rate foods. We've already seen how this led people to agriculture. Taking those lower-return-rate foods means devoting more time to the food quest or finding other sources of cheap labor, such as slaves. It means investing time in the technology needed to harvest and process lower-return-rate foods to increase their return rate, such as the technology for harvesting and grinding seeds. Many people might imagine a nomadic hunter-gatherer existence as hand-to-mouth living, a continual scramble for the next meal. Hunting and gathering isn't easy, but sedentary folks aren't let off the hook; they also must work diligently.

If nomadic foragers cope with bad times by moving, what do sedentary villages do? If all the good places are occupied and things go south, your first choice might be to mooch off the neighbors who are fortunate enough to be better situated. This was the case on North America's Northwest Coast. Sedentary hunter-gatherers there relied heavily on fall salmon runs to provide them with their winter's supply of food. Some large streams offered consistently large runs of salmon, but smaller streams had smaller runs that were more variable from year to year. The problem is that those who lived on small streams periodically needed assistance from villages sitting on the mouths of large streams, but the reverse was rarely the case.

Letting another village into your food supply will inevitably lower what's available for your village. So why do so? Why not say "let them eat cake"? I'd like to think that the better angels of our nature would get our attention, but the real reason is that starving people are desperate, and desperate people do desperate things, such as attack; letting people in, then, staves off violence.

And if you let others in, you can control what they get. Nothing compels you to give them equal shares (if the alternative is nothing, they might be grateful for anything). But the hosts have to explain this inequality. They might do so by pointing out that their guests are improvident, lazy, or stupid ("Who would put their village on such a small stream?" "Why didn't you work harder to store food?" "You don't deserve our help, but we will be magnanimous and take care of you"). As population increases, this process is repeated both within and between villages.

The Northwest Coast feasts we mentioned in the previous chapter are where people explain to themselves the relations of inequality that such situations produce. Giving away food and possessions is intended to embarrass visitors and to remind them who is the more powerful. On the Northwest Coast, a village chief acquired prestige at a feast he hosted because everyone in his village knew he had just bought off or warned off the competition.

This process set into motion the inequality that pervades the world today. Culturally, a state's elite must "explain" to themselves and to others why they should get more. This is what anthropologists call *ideologies,* belief systems that account for inequality. They permit violence on many levels, from denying people basic rights to warfare and slavery. To maintain a social order that benefits them, the elite need to consider themselves a higher class of humanity than the "riffraff" outside the Bastille, the Tower of London, or the Forbidden City, inherently more civilized, more religious, more intelligent . . . more deserving. Archaeology shows that as states spread their reach, no society in the world has been immune from oppression or from being oppressors. Some groups are classed as slaves, and women become pawns as marriages are used to create alliances. But racism and sexism do not reflect our Paleolithic nature; they are ideologies installed after the fourth beginning.[23] Their reality is as false as their effects are real.

Religion took on a new role in the ideologies of states. One way to justify inequality is to link a ruler's claim to the throne through one's god. Who could prove that Ramesses was *not* descended from a god? Or that God is *not* speaking through the Pope? Much of the history of Europe is Catholics burning Protestants or Protestants burning Catholics. Today, religious fundamentalists of various stripes try to control their country's government. This, too, is a continuation of an ancient practice of the fourth beginning.

You sit on your perch for some five thousand years, watching this drama unfold. Sometimes it's noble: writing, mathematics, astronomy, physics, metalworking, glassmaking, architecture, ship-building—the groundwork was laid for the technologies that improve our lives today. But sometimes it's pathetic: massacres, poverty, slavery, prisons, debt, war. Powers rise and fall; wars are won and lost; empires expand and contract; people alternate between being slaves and being enslavers, rich and poor, winners and losers.

. . .

In the last four chapters we've covered the highlights of world history in terms of four beginnings. With hindsight we can see that dramatic changes in the material record of humanity's odyssey on earth—stone tools, art and burials, villages, domesticated crops, elaborate tombs, palisades, temples, palaces, and so on—point to equally dramatic changes in how people related to one another. And . . . is that it? Are we at the end of history? Maybe the way things have been is not the way they are now, but perhaps you ask, are things now the way they always will be? It's a fair question. To answer it, you'll have to take a close look from your seat in the stratosphere, an honest look at the recent past, after the origin of the state, and ask, is another major shift visible *from an archaeological perspective?*

CHAPTER 7

Nothing Lasts Forever

The Fifth Beginning

Study the past if you would divine the future.
—Confucius

It was the baboons that did it, those baboons staring into the darkness.

Anthropologists aren't supposed to think that anything humans do is strange, such as talking with forest spirits while in a trance, dancing with the exhumed remains of their ancestors, or screaming obscenities at a football game while wearing a simulated cheese wedge for a hat. But get an anthropologist alone and he or she will admit that every once in a while we encounter something that makes us forget our profession, shake our heads, and mutter, "This is weird." For me, it was the baboons.

I don't mean furry baboons scampering about in the warm African sunlight. No, I mean cold, dead baboons in the catacombs of Tuna el-Gebel along the Nile.

At Tuna el-Gebel, beneath the tomb of Petosiris, lies a labyrinth of catacombs dedicated to Thoth, an Egyptian god associated with the moon, writing, magic, and knowledge. Walk along the dark passageways and you notice the walls are covered with niches, many holding tiny wooden coffins. Shine your flashlight down a side passage and the light passes over thousands of such coffins. Some are broken open, and tumbling out are the mummified remains of ibises, toothpick-legged birds with long, curving beaks, one of Thoth's icons. You know that Egyptians mummified people, but did you know they also mummified beetles, cats, fish, crocodiles, ibises, and cattle? They even mummified an elephant.

Eventually, you come upon another passage. At its far end is a stone pedestal on which rests a sculpted baboon, sitting on its haunches, its hands resting casually on its knees. As you walk toward it, you notice elaborate niches along the walls. All of them are walled up except one, and it contains a baboon, a mummified baboon, wrapped in cloth, squatting on a pedestal. And you surmise that behind each of the walled niches is another baboon sitting in silence, staring at darkness for eternity. "Weird," you mutter. "What were they thinking?"

Of course, the ancient Egyptians weren't weird. They're just hard to imagine. Yet for archaeologists, imagining other worlds is precisely the point.

Imagine sitting with a Paleolithic hunter some 15,000 years ago while you both warm yourselves at night beside a fire. You point up at the moon and tell your companion that someday men will travel there, in a rocket made of metal, powered by liquid hydrogen fuel, because the elected president of a democratic nation had pledged to make it happen. He stares at you through the flames and asks, "What's metal?" It's not only the technology that he can't imagine, but also elections, democracy, presidents, and nations. And this makes me wonder what *we* haven't imagined about our future.

. . .

In the past four chapters we've seen humans repeatedly become something completely different from what they once were. Arboreal primates did not intend to become bipedal, tool-wielding, hunting hominins. And those hominins didn't intend to become symbol-using, storytelling, spirit-conjuring humans. Nor did hunter-gatherers intend to become farmers, who, in turn, did not dream of becoming part of a voracious empire. Throughout history, we've just tried to be best at what we were: the best arboreal primate, the best tool-using hominin, the best hunter-gatherer, the best leader of an agricultural village. And yet doing so made us into something else.

Could the same thing be happening now? In trying to be the best industrial, best capitalist, best-defended society we can be, are we becoming something completely different?

It's hard to recognize a new beginning if you're part of it. No Neolithic villager woke up one morning and said, "Hey, we're all farmers now!" But we do have a record, from archaeology, of the signs of no-turning-back change. We know that past beginnings are accompanied by significant change in our physical signature on the planet—for example, stone tools, cave art, domesticated plants, and temple complexes. So let's imagine how archaeologists of 10,000 years from now would look back on today; let's treat today as we have treated prehistory.

When we do, I suspect future archaeologists will see another beginning, one initiated about A.D. 1500—the beginning of European colonization, the Industrial Revolution, capitalism, and globalization. A lot happened in the last five hundred years, but we'll look at time as archaeologists do, in a large slice. We're looking for the same sort of change in the material record that permits archaeologists to separate Basketmaker from Pueblo I sites (you'll remember them from chapter 2). In doing so, I think my colleagues ten thousand years from now will take note of several significant additions to the material record of humanity.

. . .

These archaeologists might first look to the sea, where the human presence is marked by shipwrecks. Dating them, they will find a few early ones on the bottom of the Mediterranean and along the coast of China. But thousands of others will date to after A.D. 1500: Spanish galleons, some laden with silver; whalers (like the thirty-three lost off the coast of Alaska in 1871); and modern-era vessels, such as Shackleton's *Endurance,* the *Bismarck,* the *Lusitania,* and the *Arizona.* Many of these will be found in deep water far from land, such as the *Titanic.* Future archaeologists will see these wrecks as something totally new in the material record of world history.

These archaeologists might then look to the skies. In space, human artifacts all date to no earlier than the late twentieth century. Archaeologists might still find artifacts orbiting the earth. NASA tracks these today: there are more than 21,000 objects greater than 10 cm in size, some 500,000 objects between 1 and 10 cm, and 100 trillion microsized objects, such as flecks of paint. And even if those objects have burned up in the atmosphere, archaeologists will still find artifacts on the moon, including the Soviet Union's *Luna 2* spacecraft and American lunar landing bases, rovers, and electronic equipment. They will no doubt scratch their heads over the flags, cameras, bits of space suits, hammers, tongs, and bags of feces, urine, and vomit, as well as a watchband, a tie tack, a Bible, a falcon feather, a javelin, $2 bills, golf balls, and a three-inch-tall statue. There are also human artifacts on Mars, and even on a comet.

Trade will also reveal a material change. Although archaeologists will see evidence of trade *within* continents for millennia before A.D. 1500, the evidence dating to after A.D. 1500 will point to the movement of goods *between* continents. Things manufactured in Spain appear in Southwestern pueblos, in the Andes, the Philippines, and Guam; Asian-manufactured goods appear in North America, Africa, and Europe. Archaeologists will find the detritus of transportation technology (planes, trains, and ships) as well as that of their supporting technology (shipping ports and airports). They will see that these link continents economically; in fact, they will find that the continents are literally linked together with cables.[1]

Looking at human skeletal data, archaeologists will discover that the neat geographic sorting of human genes, such as those for skin color, breaks down when they examine remains in cemeteries dating to after A.D. 1500. Dark-skinned peoples are adapted to equatorial regions, their skin's high melanin content providing protection from the sun. But after A.D. 1500 the skeletal remains of such people are found from Ushuaia, Argentina, to Tromsö, Norway, evidence of a level of human migration not seen since the world was colonized by hunter-gatherers 10,000 years earlier.

Analyzing the isotopic composition of human skeletons, archaeologists will find a similar collapse of geographic sorting after A.D. 1500. You are what you eat, and prior to A.D. 1500 everyone ate local foods, so human bones contain the carbon, nitrogen, and strontium isotopic signatures of local environments (such data are what permitted us to determine Ötzi's home). But with imported foods, many people dine daily on products from the four corners of the world. On the morning I wrote this, in Wyoming, I had a banana from Ecuador; granola made of Scottish oats; yoghurt from the milk of cows pastured in upstate New York, flavored with vanilla probably from Madagascar; and coffee grown in Columbia. The isotopic signature of my skeleton reflects not Wyoming but the world.

Archaeologists will also find evidence of global war. Spanish warships are found not only off the coast of Spain but also in the Caribbean, off the coast of South America, near Guam, and the Philippines. The same World War II artifacts that lie off the shores of Normandy also appear in Pacific lagoons, near Iwo Jima, and the Philippines. Future archaeologists will note that organic materials grown after A.D. 1945 record an oddly high carbon-14 composition; they might correctly surmise this to be the result of above-ground nuclear bomb testing.

Most of all, future archaeologists will see that the footprint of humanity increases dramatically after A.D. 1500. The city of Denver in A.D. 1850 was a small town of a few hundred people that sat alone where the prairie meets the Rocky Mountains. Only 150 years later—think of that in terms of the time span we've covered in this book—and it's a city of 650,000, embedded in Colorado's Front Range community, which stretches for 133 miles, from Fort Collins to Colorado Springs, and which is home to some 4.5 million people.

Future archaeologists might discern that in 2007, and *for the first time in human history*, the majority of the world's population lived in cities, not in rural areas. A distinguishing material characteristic of today will be the planet's twenty-eight megacities, each home to more than ten million people (the largest being Tokyo, with 38 million inhabitants).

In fact, geologists today are debating whether to adopt a new label for our time, the *Anthropocene*.[2] For the first time in world history, humanity's impact on our planet is the earth's major feature. Archaeologists will see this in evidence for a tremendous increase in the amount of energy harnessed from the earth—the ruins of hydroelectric plants, arrays of solar cells, wind turbines, and power plants. And they will see the mines to acquire energy: massive open pits, lopped-off mountain tops, and deep subterranean mines. There is nothing like them prior to A.D. 1500. On an archaeological time scale, all these features explode into existence at the same time as the first coal mines in Great Britain.

Archaeologists will similarly find massive buildings after A.D. 1500, reflecting the growing population. They might note that in 2500 B.C., the world's tallest structure was Khufu's Pyramid in Egypt, 480 feet tall. It held the record for more than four thousand years, until A.D. 1888, when the 555-foot-tall Washington monument in Washington, DC, was completed. After that, tall buildings appear overnight, in archaeological time, from the 1,063-foot-tall Eiffel Tower (1889) to the 2,717-foot-tall Burj Khalifa in Dubai (2009).

And they will notice trash. It's everywhere. They will take note of the Fresh Kills landfill on Staten Island, which was already one of the world's largest structures even before New York City interred the wreckage of the World Trade Center there. Archaeologists will find tons of trash on the Alaskan coast and figure out that a confluence of currents brings it to Alaska from Asia. They might find an island of garbage bigger than the state of Texas floating in the north Pacific; if not, they might find a very high density of microscopic plastics in the ocean. And a layer of plastic shopping bags might mark the boundary of the Anthropocene in archaeological sites just as a geologic spike in iridium records the meteor impact that killed the dinosaurs and ushered in the age of mammals 66 million years ago.

Tree rings and other data sources will record a twenty-first-century rise in atmospheric CO_2, the highest in over 800,000 years, and corals will record an increase in oceanic acidity. Archaeologists will see an increase in global temperature in tree rings and ice cores, and they will connect the dots back to fossil-fuel power plants, internal combustion engines, and domesticated animals. With the benefit of hindsight, they will see ironclad proof of the link between human actions and climate change. And they will not find earlier evidence of humanly caused climate change in our species' six-million-year history.[3]

A future archaeologist could also calculate that the speed of change in material culture vastly increased after A.D. 1500. Think, for example, of how much change occurred in the lives of Paleolithic hunter-gatherers between 25,500 and 25,000 B.C.—comparatively speaking, none. But think of the difference between A.D. 1500 and today. In fact, think of the difference between just the early twentieth and the early twenty-first centuries.

When my father was born in 1925 in Pawtucket, Rhode Island, the cool technology was the zipper (invented in 1913). Television and talking movies appeared when he was two years old, penicillin when he was three. His father ferried mail between Pawtucket and Boston in a biplane. My father's childhood icebox was, in fact, kept cold by ice, brought to his house by horse and wagon. He remembers hand-cranking a Model A. And yet he flew on the Concorde and saw men walk on the moon.

Computers didn't exist when my father was born; in fact, vacuum tubes (1910) were the latest technology, later replaced by transistors (1947), my generation's cool technology, which was in turn replaced by microchips.[4] In graduate school I wrote computer programs using punch cards, and I thought an IBM Selectric typewriter was all the technology I would ever need. I remember life before the Internet and cell phones and Apple and the "Cloud"—and I'm not that old! We take for granted that technology changes every six months, yet such rapid change is a characteristic of only this era in history.

Archaeologists will look at all these changes in the human signature on earth and know that they are looking at a period of radical change, something on the order of the beginnings of technology, the capacity for culture, agriculture, or the state—a time of great transformation, a new beginning.

. . .

In previous chapters we saw how various processes brought about significant change in human societies. We saw how trying to be one thing invariably led humans to become something completely different. And we saw that population growth was a primary driver of this process.

Future archaeologists can track evidence for a growing human population. They will discover that about 1850, and for the first time in humanity's history, world population surpassed one billion. They will also see that an uptick in the rate of growth occurred in the mid-nineteenth century, the result of advances in medicine, public health, and agricultural industrialization that reduced mortality.[5] But fertility did not decline, and the power of large numbers took over. Prior to the nineteenth century, world population probably doubled every 1,700 years; after 1850 it doubled in less than 50 years.

Since 1965, population growth has slowed in developed nations,[6] but global population will continue to rise throughout this century. The United Nations estimates world population will reach 10.3 billion by 2070, a date potentially within the lifetime of any young person today, and then decline sometime after 2100 as more nations develop and experience reduced birth rates.[7]

Looking at world history, we see that it doesn't take much population increase to spur competition for resources. Some apes dropped from the trees and crossed the savanna on two legs because there were too many arboreal competitors in the scattered forests of six million years ago. That adventurous hominin population was successful, and some, members of the genus *Homo,* spread beyond Africa. Members of that population who became cultural could create cooperative alliances that helped them weather droughts and other hard times, so their population grew. Some left Africa and outcompeted other hominins, such as the Neanderthals. The cost of that success was competition for living space, eventually resulting in agriculture. Farming locked people onto land, and some members found they had to control the resources and labor of others to survive, and being clever cultural beings, they came up with ideologies to justify the military control of their world and the subjugation of their neighbors.

Knowing that population growth played an important role in past beginnings and that growth will continue throughout this century, we draw the logical conclusion: we are about to witness another dramatic change in human organization. The material record of the past five hundred years is a further sign of coming change. It's the fifth beginning, the end of the world as we know it. But don't worry; we've been through this before.

. . .

What might the fifth beginning bring? There is an old Danish proverb: "Never make predictions, especially about the future."[8] That's good advice, because futurists are usually wrong. In fact, the computer scientist Alan Kay once said, "The best way to predict the future is to create it."[9] Therefore, I won't claim what *will* happen, but, informed by the expanse of human history, I will describe trends that jointly point to what *should* happen.

Most people think about the future in terms of technology: self-driving cars, personal drones, implanted technology . . . who knows? Maybe we'll make purchases through a DNA-linked financial account (as envisioned by David Poyer in his novel *Stepfather Bank*), or maybe we'll inject nanobots into our bloodstreams to cure diseases, as futurist Ray Kurzweil predicts.[10] I think neurologically integrated prostheses would be a marvel, and I'd really appreciate a device that downloads information directly to my brain (as in *The Matrix*). Some look forward to the *singularity,* when humans and machines merge (as in the unsettling Borg of *Star Trek*).

Although technology will of course be integral to our future lives, as an archaeologist I'm more interested in changes in human organization, in how people relate to one another. The real challenge lies not in new technology but in new ways to organize ourselves. We could discuss many things, but I'll focus on a question many people ask: will we have a world government?

Usually, a discussion of world government conjures up frightful images—black helicopters and mind police, Ray Bradbury's *Fahrenheit 451*, George Orwell's *1984*, or Philip K. Dick's *Minority Report*.[11] Are these visions correct, or is it that world government is as difficult for members of nation-states to imagine as metal or space travel would be for a Paleolithic hunter?

Some social scientists have tried to predict when we might have a world government. To do so, they examine trends in the size of the world's largest political entity over time. Prior to the breakup of the Soviet Union, the world seemed to be on a steady trend: the size of the largest political entity—country, if you prefer—became larger over time. Following the trajectory out, these researchers predicted a single world political entity anywhere from a few hundred to a few thousand years from now.[12]

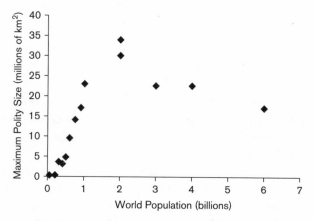

FIGURE 4. The relationship between population growth and the size of the largest single political unit ("polity") on earth over the past three thousand years. The decline since the world's population hit two billion is a product of the breakup of the Soviet Union and other countries. Y-axis data from Carneiro (2004); Peregrine, Ember, and Ember (2004); Roscoe (2004); and Taagepera (1978).

But time isn't what causes large-scale change. As we've seen in previous chapters, change has to do with technology, climate, environment—and especially population. And the number of people on earth is growing exponentially. Figure 4 shows the size of the world's largest political entity graphed against estimates of world population size for the past three thousand years. (We don't have good data prior to that date, but we know early political entities were small.) A single world polity would encompass about 133 million square kilometers (all the earth's land minus Greenland and Antarctica). Had we analyzed these data when the world's population stood below 3 billion, we would have reached a startling conclusion: we would have expected humanity to forge a single country at a world population of 7.6 billion, or, at the current rate of growth, by the year A.D. 2020.[13] In other words, now.

But it's imprudent to use a simple empirical pattern for predictions, and the figure shows why: the size of the largest political entity has declined with recent population growth. The late twentieth century saw a steady *increase* in the number of countries as colonial powers let go of their holdings, as the Soviet Union divided, and as some countries fragmented (e.g., Sudan, Yugoslavia, Czechoslovakia). Extrapolating from the growth in independent states over time, we might predict that today's 196 countries could be over 300 by the end of this century.[14] But do the last few decades override the trend of the previous three thousand years? Are they merely a blip in the data?

Our examination of world prehistory provides us with practice at discerning the significant, albeit invisible processes at work behind the chart. These are processes that seek to maintain an existing adaptation but that contain the seeds of transformative change. Three processes speak to the apparently contradictory trends of the twentieth century and point to the future of a world government: capitalism's search for cheap labor, the arms race, and the globalization of human culture.

. . .

Capitalism is a logical outgrowth of our long-standing evolutionary desire to ensure our survival. It's people trying to guarantee survival by controlling the necessities of life, which in capitalist systems means maximizing profit. Labor is one of a manufacturer's highest costs, and owners seek to maximize profit by reducing the cost of labor.

One way to reduce labor's cost is through technology. The Industrial Revolution, powered largely by coal and the steam engine, was a great technological leap, and it took hold because it helped increase profits by replacing workers with cheaper machines. James Watt's steam engine, for example, helped power textile mills and increased productivity enormously—by replacing people.[15] Capitalism began a process of mechanization and assembly lines; manufacturing robotics are only the latest in this trend.

Don't misunderstand me. I worked briefly on a newspaper production line in college and have no desire to return to such dull, repetitive, backbreaking labor. But the downside to labor's replacement is that those "freed" from such menial labor have to find another way to live. People are pushed out of capitalist industries just as some apes were pushed out of the trees. In Britain, for example, the agricultural labor force dropped from 75 to 35 percent of the population between A.D. 1500 and 1800.[16] The need to enlist more people into the state's service (e.g., as a standing army) demanded efficiencies in agriculture that dropped labor needs further. For many years, the percentage of the labor force in developed nations involved in food production has been in the single digits.

In the past, labor-freeing technological advances opened new areas of employment, generally after a period of disruption as those advances reset the economy. But some economists worry that trend might not continue. In 2015, the proportion of adults in the current American labor force was at its lowest since 1978, and many of those employed

are in part-time, underpaid jobs.[17] We have yet to see if the late twenti-
eth-century shift from a predominantly manufacturing to a predominantly service industry will generate decent employment.

Capitalism also used more nefarious ways to reduce labor costs,
including slavery, child labor, and indentured servitude. The economy
of the American South, which supplied cotton to textile mills, depended
on slave labor. Child labor was a substantial part of the textile and coal
industries in Britain until the mid-nineteenth century. In the United
States of the early twentieth century, coal miners indebted to the com-
pany store were, in essence, held captive, and strikes often resulted in
pitched battles, as at Ludlow, Colorado in 1914.

Worker protection laws and unions eventually caught up and raised
the cost of labor. The response was to send manufacturing jobs overseas, where labor was cheaper. In the United States, this began in earnest after World War II, when we outsourced labor to Japan and elsewhere, notably in the electronics industry.[18] Today the Internet permits
even nonmanufacturing labor to go overseas. Companies in the United
States and Europe can send their books to accountants in India, which
is also where many of the world's call centers are located.[19]

Nonetheless, for all its effort to reduce labor costs, capitalism slowly
but inevitably raises living standards. Since World War II the middle
class has expanded in Japan, Singapore, South Korea, and now in India
and China. As living standards rise, so too does the cost of labor. When
it does, companies maximize profit by moving to the next cheapest
source. Capitalism has succeeded as long as there has been another
cheap pool of labor. But the world is finite and so that process was
always destined to draw to a close; cheap labor will eventually disappear. Parts of Asia and much of Africa still have not been tapped, but
that will change quickly in the coming decades. In fact, Africa is seeing
an enormous influx of capital (notably from China).[20]

Maybe capitalism will shift to industries that can't be so easily relo-
cated, such as tourism or service industries (e.g., child care, hospice,
health care), and to industries that profit by correcting our errors—
recycling, trash repurposing, installing renewable energy in households,
and environmental reconstruction. But the larger question is, what will
happen to capitalism when the world's cheap labor is gone?

. . .

The arms race did not begin with the Cold War but with state societies
some five thousand years ago. Your enemy builds a spear, so you build

a shield. They build a crossbow, so you build a castle. They build a catapult, so you build cannons. They build machine guns, so you build tanks and poisonous gas. They build submarines and long-range bombers, so you build nuclear weapons.

This escalation entails a spiraling cost. A bow and arrow is cheap; a castle costs more. A P-51 Mustang fighter aircraft built in 1944 cost about $675,000 in today's money. That's expendable technology.[21] But the latest in airborne warfare, the F-35 fighter, costs $135 million each, and each B-2 stealth bomber costs over $800 million. That's not expendable technology; in fact, you'd almost be afraid to use it. Maintaining nuclear capacity in the United States costs some $20 billion a year, even with our reduced arsenal. The tab for the wars in Iraq and Afghanistan is nearly $2 trillion.[22] The cost of weapon systems and war spirals ever upwards; it has for the past five thousand years. And yet these costly instruments of destruction often are obsolete before they are used. I live about fifty miles from some of the nation's original ICBM silos—which today are being decommissioned, dismantled, and filled with concrete, never having fired a single missile.[23]

This expensive technology deters aggressors, but James Fallows points out that while "technology is our military's main advantage . . . the story of the post 9/11 'long wars' is of America's higher-tech advantages yielding transitory victories that melt away before the older, messier realities of improvised weapons, sectarian resentments, and mounting hostilities."[24] I'm *not* advocating it, but one wonders why we don't use our military's full awesome might? Why didn't we bomb Iraq "back to the Stone Age"? Why didn't we use nuclear weapons on Afghanistan?

We didn't for two reasons. First, it would have left an expensive mess for us to clean up. Second, we didn't because of a significant cultural shift in the Western world. The Western world expects to live in peace and won't accept casualties of the kind we accepted, for example, as the cost of victory on D-Day in 1944. Neither will it accept collateral damage, such as the accidental bombing of an Afghani wedding party or hospital. A country today cannot carpet-bomb civilians (e.g., as we did in Dresden, Tokyo, and Vietnam), to say nothing of using nuclear weapons, without paying a large political price both internally and externally. The late John Keegan wrote in *A History of Warfare* that war

> may well be ceasing to commend itself to human beings as a desirable, or productive, let alone rational, means of reconciling their discontents. This is not mere idealism. Mankind does have the capacity, over time, to correlate

the costs and benefits of large and universal undertakings. Throughout much of the time for which we have a record of human behavior, mankind can clearly be seen to have judged that war's benefits outweighed its costs, or appeared to do so when a putative balance was struck. Now the computation works in the opposite direction. Costs clearly exceed benefits.[25]

The war machine simply costs too much in the modern era: in technology that can't be used, in postwar reconstruction, and in lives. It also costs too much in our empathetic agony over the suffering of others. This trend may have begun with the Vietnam War, the first televised war, and continues today with immediate, uncensored images of the full human horror of war. There is a cultural disconnect between what the Western world expects life to be (peaceful, prosperous) and what it actually often is (not peaceful, not prosperous). Paleolithic artists tried to resolve similar conundrums by painting on cave walls.

The technology of war has brought us to an important Rubicon. We want bad guys brought to justice, but we don't want hospitals to be bombed. The Western world is stuck in a bind: it can't use the full power of its military without violating its own cultural expectations. War no longer works.

Yet the world remains a dangerous place. After grabbing the Crimea in 2014, Russia's president Putin showed that a nuclear power can push its neighbors around. As Putin reminded the world on television, no one will risk conflict with a nuclear power because even if that power loses, it might first decimate New York, Paris, Beijing, or London. At the other end of the spectrum, terrorists have shown how they can subvert powerful militaries by going "underneath" them, by flying commandeered commercial jets into buildings or by using social media to turn a country's disgruntled citizens against itself. Terrorists act with impunity because they know the cultural conundrum the Western world faces.

Standing on the Uruk plain in southern Iraq five thousand years ago, when the arms race began in earnest, we might have predicted all this. Our technological cleverness made it inevitable that the arms race would lead to the point where war cannot solve the problems it is intended to solve. Yet disputes are not ending. What will replace war as a problem-solving device?

. . .

This brings us to a third, and related, process: the effects of globalization. In 2014, Scotland came close to voting to secede from the United Kingdom, and in 2016, the United Kingdom voted to leave the European

Union. The Kurds want their own country carved out of Iraq. Flanders wishes to break away from Belgium, some Venetians wish to secede from Italy, Brittany grumbles about leaving France, the Basques and Catalonians want to secede from Spain, the Quebecois mutter about leaving Canada, and Russian separatists seek to break from Ukraine. The Islamic State seeks its own medieval heaven in Syria and Iraq. The Moros in the Philippines want an autonomous region, as do the Uighurs in China. Many diplomats see a two-state solution in Palestine as the only possible outcome of the Israeli-Palestinian conflict. And Texas is not the only U.S. state to murmur about secession.[26]

Clamoring for autonomy is a predictable response to globalization. Recall that culture entails a symbolic construction of the world, an account of how things should be. Whether it's right or wrong is inconsequential: culture is what allows us to make sense of the world. Take someone's culture away, and they are left spinning. If you've traveled overseas and experienced culture shock, you know what I'm talking about. You have that vague, indefinable sense that something's not right; culture shock can even produce physical illness and depression.

The global communication and trade technology created by capitalism brings Western culture into the lives of everyone in the world. And many, such as members of Boko Haram in Nigeria, find the mere presence of other cultures to be a threat. People who fear foreign cultures cite specific disagreements (such as the education of women), but for others, the mere hint that one's understanding of the world might not be right is upsetting. Religion often becomes the idiom for violent push-back, but it's not the real cause of violence.[27] Today we point the finger at Islamic fundamentalists, but it was not so long ago (in an archaeologist's timescale) that Catholics and Protestants went to war in Europe.

And it's not just Islamists who fear loss of the "old ways." Our culture is essential to our sense of self, to guiding us through each day. Unfortunately, this means that any critique of one's culture can sound as if you're throwing down a gauntlet. You've no doubt heard something like "Those bureaucrats in Washington are attacking our way of life; they don't understand our values." It might entail private property, wolves, guns, abortion, coal, same-sex marriage, logging, or fracking, but it's really a difference in cultural values, values that become grounds for anger because our culture is a large part of who we are. Suggest to some people that their culture is wrong, and they will retaliate, possibly with force, because they want the world to make sense, and they make sense of the world through culture. This is a predictable result of the rapid and pervasive penetration of information from other cultures brought about by the global economic system.

Benjamin Barber described this situation in *Jihad versus McWorld*.[28] It's a battle between "traditional" cultures and a growing "transnational," Western-dominated culture. One manifestation is religious, national, and ethnic fanaticism. Hindu nationalism, for example, is on the rise in India just as that nation becomes a major player in the world's economy and is exposed to more Western culture. Members of such movements often seek to break away from the mother country and the purportedly "evil influences" that have captured it and return to an earlier "proper" world. Islamic fundamentalists seek to return to a caliphate, and the Tea Party seeks to return the United States to its perception of the country's roots.[29] We are in the middle of many revitalization movements, of the kind we described in chapter 1.[30]

In any case, blowback, including political fragmentation, is the inevitable result of globalization. So here's the challenge: how can we integrate the world's peoples economically, legislatively, structurally—and fairly—without forcing them to change culturally?

. . .

Is there any light at the end of the tunnel that is not an oncoming train? Yes. In each of the past four beginnings, humanity devised new levels of cooperation: pair-bonding, sharing, alliances, trade. This beginning is no different. At the same time that war has become less useful, as capitalism has undermined its future viability, and as globalization has brought about a clash of cultures, the twentieth century has also witnessed some of the largest cooperative ventures of human history. I am speaking here of entities that crosscut nation-states, entities that are similar to what anthropologists call *sodalities* (from the Latin *sodalitat*, meaning "comradeship"). If I had to write an essay on what happened in the twentieth century (remember that five-hundred-word assignment from chapter 2?), this would be my focus.[31]

In anthropology, sodalities are social groups that crosscut what otherwise are competitive kinship units, such as lineages and clans. They include age grades (groups of boys or girls of about the same age) or religious organizations such as the religious kiva groups of Southwestern pueblos. Their function, from an anthropological point of view, is to reduce the likelihood of dangerous schisms between kinship groups, to create ties that bind. They are Kiwanis and Rotary Clubs, fraternal organizations, and even bowling leagues. Members of these groups might compete with one another, but sodalities reduce that competition's potential for harm.

In the past century global, sodality-like entities included the League of Nations, the United Nations, the Council of Europe, the European Union, NATO, the World Trade Organization, the World Court, the International Monetary Fund, the G-8, non-governmental organizations (NGOs), and even global religions. Africa has started the East African Community to coordinate economic and other relations. There is NAFTA the Trans-Pacific Partnership and the proposed Transatlantic Trade and Investment Partnership.

Such organizations and agreements couldn't exist without the technology that allows people and information to circle the globe rapidly, so they are linked to the technological advances that were driven by the capitalist economic system, advances whose purpose was not to promote cooperation but to reap large profits. Likewise, they are driven by the desire to reduce warfare by relieving the cause of disagreements; the threat of nuclear annihilation was a crucial impetus. They are also driven by the need to cleave together people who must work with each other but who have fundamentally very different perspectives on life. In other words, capitalism, war, and the globalization of culture create the need for a new level of cooperation.

As I pointed out in the first chapter, those who study evolution know that acts of altruism and cooperation often arise because they are beneficial to the competitive process. We cooperate to compete; in business jargon it's known as *co-opetition*. But as capitalism taps out the world's cheap labor and business becomes even more global, as war loses its capacity to do anything other than suck up vast amounts of resources, and as the global economy creates an inescapable clash of cultures, we could reach a tipping point where we compete at cooperation.[32]

What might this mean for nations?

. . .

Some years ago, General James Cartwright, former vice-chairman of the Joints Chief of Staff, argued that "mankind's central organizing construct for the last 350 years has been the nation-state [but] . . . the information age has eroded" its powers by facilitating "the free flow of people, capital, and information across borders. . . . Traditional alliances between Nation-States struggle to remain relevant [and] traditional organizational structures designed during the industrial age to provide stability by gaining and maintaining advantage will be challenged."[33]

Boundaries mean little to multinational corporations, which today act almost like sodalities, because war and poverty are generally bad for business (unless you're in the arms business). Globalization expert Parag Khanna argues that this economic process will fragment nations as regions and cities find their best economic alternative is to negotiate their own relations with trading partners.[34] He suggests these might be "parastates," or "special economic zones" located within nations; megacities will probably be the first such zones. This is already happening, and the United Nations sees a "nonstate" world as a viable scenario in as little as a generation.

However, those smaller entities will be unable to maintain their own defense, both physical and economic. Assuming that disputes will continue, what will resolve them if war has proven to be ineffectual?

One mechanism comes from our hunter-gatherer ancestors: sanctions that entail shunning and ostracism. In the modern world, such sanctions must have monetary value, of the kind the United States and Europe imposed on Russia for its intervention in Ukraine in 2014. If war is no longer viable, then the need to "do something" about rule breakers (especially nuclear-armed ones) might have brought us to a tipping point.

Sanctions work only if they are strong, and that implies a cost to those doing the sanctioning. The cost may be too high if only one or a few countries impose sanctions (this is why President Obama once said that the United States could no longer be the world's policeman). If spread across numerous countries, the cost to any individual country would be so low that cooperation in sanctioning would be likely.

If countries continue to break apart or separate into autonomous or semiautonomous regions, the need for an overarching body to coordinate punishment will be felt even more keenly, because what kind of army or financial sanctions could an independent Flanders, for example, muster on its own? In other words, if all nations were small, we'd have no choice but to cooperate. Khanna could be right that "yet more fragmentation and division, even new sovereign states, are a crucial step in a longer process toward building transnational stability among neighbors."[35]

. . .

Existing nation-states will oppose this vision of political and economic evolution because culture has elevated the nation-state to a sacred status. Listen to the rhetoric in almost any of the world's trouble spots and you will hear the words "sovereign state." The United States heard them after it invaded Iraq. China said the same in response to criticism of its human rights record. (And we hear it within the United States as well. In 2015 Senator Lisa Murkowski called President Obama's decision to cease oil drilling in the Alaska National Wildlife Preserve "a stunning attack on our sovereignty."[36])

Politicians would tell you that one country simply cannot interfere in the affairs of a "sovereign state." The Australian jurist H. V. Evatt once said that "sovereignty is neither a question of fact, nor a question of law, but a question that does not arise at all."[37] If this were true, then the concept of a nation-state as something special should be eternal, but you know it's not. The state is a recent invention in human history. Upper Paleolithic hunter-gatherers and Neolithic farmers would have found the concept unintelligible.

In fact, historians trace the idea of the sacred nation-state to the 1648 Peace of Westphalia (this is why General Cartwright gave the nation-state only 350 years of influence). The Peace of Westphalia entailed treaties among several European entities, treaties that arranged boundaries, settled disputes, and established the legitimacy of (some) religions. Its legacy was the importance of each political entity's sovereign rule over its internal affairs. The idea of sovereignty was actually a convenient ideology to consolidate some individuals' power grabs, and it didn't stop violations—in fact, the following centuries saw many (think Napoleon and Hitler). But it did create the cultural sense that these actions were immoral.

Global interconnections and dependencies have now changed the game. Trade imbalances and political instability cause laborers to migrate from poor to wealthy countries. The carbon spewed into the atmosphere by China, India, and the United States affects everyone. Some futurists doubt that a world governing body can form without the presence of a common enemy; as in the film *Independence Day* this would have to be nasty extraterrestrials. But it's possible that climate change and environmental degradation could be that common "enemy," one that also forces a new level of cooperation.

. . .

Climate change is like the long freight trains full of coal that rumble through my home state: put the brakes on and it will still take a long time to stop. For the long term, we need a solution, but for the short term (and that's what most people care about) we need to adapt to climate change's effects.

Climate change will affect us through rising sea levels, extreme weather events, and local drought. Globally, about two hundred million people live on land below five meters in elevation, and many of them will be displaced by rising sea levels. Some island nations, such as the Maldives and the Marshall Islands, will simply disappear beneath the waves. Coastal nations such as Bangladesh and the Netherlands and cities such as New York, Miami, New Orleans, London, and Shanghai will either have to be depopulated or pay enormous costs for protection.[38] You might think that sea level rise will be slow and that cities will simply adapt through gradual abandonment. But before sea level reaches its maximum height, whatever that may be, a hurricane or tsunami is likely to create a massive refugee population overnight (as Hurricane Katrina did). While some areas might see increased precipitation (as water is freed from melting ice), others will see drought. People fight when there's no food; in fact, historical studies show tight links between climate change, especially drought, and conflict,[39] and the Pentagon cites climate change as a coming security threat.

Populations will be displaced by rising sea levels and drought, as well as by war. Where will they go? Who will take them in? Just like those hunter-gatherers who once lived in villages on North America's Northwest Coast, some will need the resources of other nations—jobs and a place to live—but those nations will see no benefit to letting them in (we saw this happen as Syrian refugees flooded Europe in 2015). The cost of climate- and war-induced immigration will be increased border controls as well as the cost of watching humanity suffer, unless the world cooperates and devises a plan to harbor those who will be, or already have been, displaced.

Can the world actually cooperate? It could, but it won't happen easily. In *The Parliament of Man* Paul Kennedy argues that the United Nations is our best incubator for such global cooperation. In *Winning the War on War*, Joshua Goldstein points out that UN peacekeeping forces are getting better at their task, and they do it for a fraction of the cost of nations maintaining their own armies. By becoming a third party in disputes, the United Nations absolves any one nation of responsibility (another reason why the United States should not be the world's policeman).[40]

The United Nations recognized this possibility in 2005, when it passed the "responsibility to protect" doctrine, which obligates world powers to intervene when a country's leaders are destroying their own people. It stipulates times when "sovereignty" can be ignored: "The duty to prevent and halt genocide and mass atrocities lies first and foremost with the State, but the international community has a role that cannot be blocked by the invocation of sovereignty. Sovereignty no longer exclusively protects States from foreign interference." The United Nations has yet to actually implement this doctrine, but the mere fact that its members could put it in writing is an important first step.

But for the United Nations to become what it could be, it will need to reorganize, if not do away with, the Security Council. With its five permanent members (the United States, Russia, China, France and the United Kingdom), the Council was created in order to get buy-in from the post–World War II powers, none of which wanted to participate in an organization that could trump control of "their" part of the world. But any one of them can control the actions of the United Nations through veto power. That's fine if they will always be "good actors," but the track record so far leaves much to be desired. It's time for the United Nations to "cowboy up," as we say in Wyoming, and create the structure it needs to be a force for good in the world.[41] For that to happen, wealthy nations such as the United States must support it.

. . .

Ideally, world cultures would maintain peace and prosperity by themselves. As an anthropologist I see another trend, one that might be a harbinger of the kind of global cultural shift that should happen.

Global interconnectivity and rapid information transfer is creating a world culture, a new symbolically constructed understanding of humanity. This shifting culture is evidenced by a new kind of sodality-like organization, the "without borders" groups. The first of these was Doctors Without Borders, formed in 1971; it was followed by Engineers, MBAs, Reporters, Lawyers, Mediators, and Libraries Without Borders. These groups comprise people who may be quite proud of their country but who see more similarities than differences between themselves and others. This is evidence of a cultural shift toward world citizenship. We also see it in Habitat for Humanity, Amnesty International, Human Rights Watch, Greenpeace, the World Wildlife Fund, the Global Citizens Initiative, the World Citizen Foundation, and Global Citizen, among others. We see it in educational and scientific exchanges, in the Olympics, and in the international space station.

Such groups and ventures have been around for more than a century, and that may be cause to dismiss them. Just before World War I, in fact, many thought we were on the verge of world peace. In retrospect, that seems a pitiful claim. But not when you're an archaeologist who looks at the big picture: The transition has been taking place over the past five thousand years, not the past century. It will take a while longer to complete. In the meantime, we should do what we can to accelerate it.

The concept of world citizenship can be traced back to Greek philosophers such as Diogenes and Socrates. It runs through the thoughts and actions of Immanuel Kant, Adam Smith, Thomas Paine, Woodrow Wilson, Albert Einstein, Eleanor Roosevelt, and Albert Schweitzer. It shows up in Americans who saw little difference between the folks in New Orleans after Hurricane Katrina and the people in India and Indonesia after the 2004 tsunami. These globally minded citizens are few today. Maybe they are a flash in the pan, but prehistory shows that all serious change starts small. Think about it: Some three million years ago one hominin picked up a rock and saw a potential in it that no other hominin had seen. Nothing's been the same since.

A new generation is rising whose culture consists of the nonlocal, the transnational. Through smart phones, people have access to virtually all the world's information at their fingertips. E-mail and cell phones allow us to communicate in real time with people almost anywhere. Travel is more possible than it has ever been and is, as Mark Twain said, "fatal to prejudice, bigotry, and narrow-mindedness."[42] The world is interconnected; we cannot divorce ourselves from the lives of others.

The entertainment and sports industries play a special role by forming the shared experience that is crucial to the construction of culture. Jackie Chan, for example, makes movies for a world audience. The first one I saw was in 1995 in a dirt-floored, corrugated-tin-wall building in Toliara, Madagascar. The seats were rough-hewn planks set on top of cut logs. The TV and VCR were powered by a generator whose roar drowned out the sound, which was fine, because no one understood the actors' Mandarin. But everyone enjoyed the slapstick, the plot (what there was of it), and the sheer novelty.[43] Sports and music perform the same role. The World Cup is a global shared experience, and is there anyone who doesn't know who Beyoncé is? Although some governments try to shut down social media, it's impossible to do so. A million years ago, the future of humanity lay with hominins holding stone tools in their hands; today it lies with soccer-playing, Internet-surfing fourteen-year-olds holding iPhones.

. . .

Population growth has driven change in the past, and we can expect the anticipated growth of the coming century to drive change in the future. Although conflict will continue for some time, war should disappear as we come to realize that it can no longer do its job and that we can no longer afford its cost. Ten thousand years from now, archaeologists will look on the world of the twenty-first century as we look on prehistory, and they will find it hard to imagine. Perhaps when they excavate the ruins of Wyoming's ICBM missile silos or the shantytowns of Rio de Janeiro, they'll ask, "What were they thinking?"

Poverty, racism, sexism, climate change, jihad—some days the problems facing humanity seem insurmountable. But an archaeological perspective on six million years of human evolution tells us that the way things are today is not the way things always will be. The combined effect of capitalism, war, and global communication are producing world citizens. Such citizens will arise not from any legislation but as the world's population continues to interact through technology, education, the arts, sports, trade, war, and religion.[44] They should be far more amenable to the notion of a world government than are people today.

Change can happen in unpredictable ways. Few in 1980 predicted that the Berlin Wall would fall before the decade was out or that the Soviet Union would collapse. Likewise, no one in 2000 could have predicted that the United States would have an African American president by 2008. "The arc of the moral universe is long," Martin Luther King Jr. said, "but it bends toward justice." Likewise, the arc of history is long, but it bends toward unity. It has already moved strongly in that direction. And it's not what we imagined it to be. There are no black helicopters, and we have not become robots. It's not Orwell's *1984*. Let's call it "global self-governance."

. . .

Archaeologists imagine the past, but all of us must now imagine the future. That's not easy, but we must do it, for there are two things that make the fifth beginning different from previous ones.

First, humans now have the capacity to change the world. Paleolithic hunter-gatherers altered their environments by burning off grasses;

Neolithic farmers changed local vegetation maps; and Egypt's pharaohs moved mountains of rock. But none had the capacity that we do today. In his 1920 poem "Fire and Ice," Robert Frost wondered how we would use our power to destroy the world. But there's a hopeful spin on Frost's musings: if we have the power to destroy the world, then perhaps we also have the power to create it. This means geoengineering and new ways to produce, store, transmit, and use energy. But it also means devising new ways to organize ourselves, ways that will release the best in us and restrain the worst. That is a difficult task, but not an impossible one.

Second, we have history to educate us. The Paleolithic hunter could not imagine a world different from the one he roamed; what evidence was there that it *could* be different? The Neolithic farmer could not look over the Tigris-Euphrates and envision the nation-state of Iraq, much less a Green Zone, the "Islamic State," or the United Nations. Those who stood atop the Pyramid of the Moon at Teotihuacán in Mexico could not envision traveling to the moon, nor could they envision human rights, or democracy, or freedom of religion. These people knew little about the changes their ancestors had gone through, so they had little reason to think the world could be different. For them, the way things were was the way things always had been and the way things always would be. But we know better. Nothing lasts forever. Not nation-states, not a fossil-fuel-driven economy, not open-ended capitalism, and not massive inequalities in wealth.

The only open question is whether we use our capacity and knowledge to play a trick on evolution, take charge of our future and achieve the fifth beginning the easy way or the hard way. For the first time since primates dropped out of the trees and flaked a stone into a tool, human evolution *could* be, *should* be, *must* be up to us.

Notes

CHAPTER 1: THE END OF THE WORLD AS WE KNOW IT

1. Cooperative arrangements arise as part of the competitive process. For discussion of the evolution of cooperation, see Cronk and Leech (2013).

2. In fact, a more significant date might be October 13, 4772. That's when yet another Maya cycle of time, known as a p'itkun (20 b'ak'tuns), comes to a close.

3. See McKibben (1989); Fukuyama (1992); Postman (1995); Horgan (1996); D'Souza (1996); Roberts (2004); Harris (2004); Clover (2004); Sachs (2005); Rifkin (1995); Roberts (2008); Suskind (2008); Kessler (2009); Heinberg (2011); Baker (2011); Wolman (2012); Greco (2009); Horgan (2012); Rosin (2012); Carswell (2012); and Boggs (2000);

4. Diamond (2012); Wilson (2002, 2012, 2014).

5. Other than the ubiquitous self-help, diet, and management books, which are annoyingly upbeat. At least we'll all be fit, feel good about ourselves, and manage our time well as the Four Horsemen bear down upon us.

6. Kaplan (1996).

7. Hardoon, Ayele, and Fuentes-Nieva (2016). And such concentration of wealth results in a concentration of political power as well.

8. Gore (2013); Kissinger (2014); Kaplan (1996).

9. Kolbert (2014); Klein (2015); Vince (2014); Weisman (2014); Oreskes and Conway (2014); Steffen, Broadgate, et al. (2015); Steffen, Richardson, et al. (2015).

10. Weisman (2014).

11. Wright (2000); Ridley (2010); Pinker (2012); Kenny (2012); Goldstein (2012); Deaton (2013); and Ackerman (2014). See also Human Security Report Project (2011).

CHAPTER 2: HOW ARCHAEOLOGISTS THINK

1. For information on Ötzi, see Fleckinger (2003) and Fowler (2000).
2. For a biography of Crawford, see Hauser (2008).
3. Rathje and Murphy (2001).

CHAPTER 3: STICKS AND STONES

1. Harmand et al. (2015). Some animal bones dated to 3.6 million years appear to have stone tool cut marks on them. This could push the inception of stone tool technology back earlier than 3.3 million years, but whether these cut marks were indeed made by stone tools is debated.

2. Bonobos were at one time called "pygmy chimpanzees"; they are a separate species (*Pan paniscus*) from the better-known "common chimpanzee" (*Pan troglodytes*).

3. For a wonderful read on what this statement means and what it doesn't mean, see Marks (2002).

4. Napier (1970).

5. This is known as the efficient walker hypothesis; see Rodman and McHenry (1980); for an overview of different theories of bipedalism, see Vaughan (2003). Another hypothesis, proposed by Owen Lovejoy (1988), sees bipedalism as part of a complex of traits, including a shortened gestation period, increased competition, and long periods to maturation. Among many monkeys and apes, males compete for sexual access to females but don't care for the resulting offspring, which can require years to raise to maturity. Lovejoy argued that a male could have a competitive advantage if he provisioned a female and her young. To do so, he would need to carry food, and thus selection could favor bipedal males, who pass the trait on to all their offspring. Changes in pelvic structure that permitted bipedalism, however, would have required earlier birth (by reducing the size of the birth canal) and thus created infants even more dependent on an adult, presumably the mother. This could have created a feedback loop encouraging even more provisioning by males.

Although I favor the efficient walker hypothesis, it does raise a question: if bipedalism is so good for life on the savanna, why don't lions, hyenas, antelopes, wildebeests, and so forth walk around on two legs? The answer is that evolution has to build on what already exists. The body of a branch-walking ape required many genetic alterations, but far fewer than the body of, say, a lion or wildebeest. Four legs also permit greater speed than two legs, an advantage for a predator seeking to run down four-legged prey.

6. Toth and Schick (2009).

7. Thieme (1997). This find was made possible by extraordinary conditions of preservation. My sense is that whatever the earliest evidence archaeologists have for a particular technology or behavior, such as hunting, that technology or behavior had been present long before the age of the earliest evidence. This is especially true for evidence based on organic materials, such as spears. I assume, then, that this earliest evidence for hunting tells us only that large-game hunting was present by 300,000 years ago and was probably present much earlier.

8. Moura and Lee (2004). Tapping into tubers and other below-surface storage organs of geophytes as a food source could have given some hominin species a strong selective advantage. Deep storage organs are not used by many species so there is less competition for them, and they are available in dry seasons, when above-ground food sources might be scarce and competition for them intense. Like Darwin's long-billed finches, some hominins might have found an untapped food source in geophytes.

9. Maybe *H. habilis;* some label *H. habilis* and *H. rudolfensis* as australopithecines, and others consider *A. garhi* to be ancestral to the *Homo* genus. Discussion of the evolutionary relationships among the different "species" that make up human evolution is not a free-for-all, but to the uninformed it can certainly seem like it. The time period between two million and four million years ago is especially complex and, from the paleoanthropologist's point of view, unsettled. It's clear, though, that hominins at this time underwent adaptive specialization, and at least one of those hominins used tools.

10. Ungar (2004, 2012). Analysis of the animal remains from some sites points to hunting of at least small game by about two million years ago; see Ferraro et al. (2013).

11. Walker and Leakey (1993). The age at death is debated, an earlier estimate putting it at eleven years. Nariokotome also had a diseased spine, which may have contributed to his early death. Some sources classify Nariokotome as *Homo ergaster* (see footnote 16).

12. Wrangham (2009); Gowlett and Wrangham (2013); Zink and Lieberman (2016).

13. Aiello and Wheeler (1995).

14. Berna et al. (2011). This is also a hotly debated topic, but careful studies of the "micro-stratigraphy" of burned features still find little evidence of intentional hearths prior to about 400,000 years ago.

15. Ferring et al. (2011).

16. The remains of early *Homo* found outside of Africa are often classified as *Homo erectus,* whereas those found in Africa are *Homo ergaster.* We once thought these two geographic groups of hominins were sufficiently different from each other that they merited a different species classification and that *Homo ergaster* evolved into *Homo erectus.* However, a recent find from the Dmanisi site in the Republic of Georgia suggests that these different species may be just variations within one species. See Lordkipanidze et al. (2013). How the terms are used today is in a state of flux.

17. Since our spine and pelvis were originally designed for four-legged locomotion, bipedalism also created a host of other problems that continue to plague humans, including back problems such as slipped disks, as well as bunions, hernias, knee problems, and poor blood circulation.

18. Lee (1980).

CHAPTER 4: BEADS AND STORIES

1. The subject of modern human origins has been hotly debated for the past thirty years; see Bräuer (2014) and Stringer (2014) for recent reviews. In part

this is a debate over the difference between anatomically modern humans and behaviorally modern humans. Anatomically modern humans can be traced back to about 160,000 years in Africa; skeletal remains of that age are referred to as "archaic *Homo sapiens*" because their skulls look different enough from those of *Homo erectus* to label them something different, but not similar enough to modern humans to just call them *Homo sapiens*. Fossils that are less than 200,000 years old, however, are similar enough to modern humans to classify them with modern humans.

2. Mithen (1996).

3. See Kaminski (2014) for a review. Only humans seem to know when another's thoughts are false or conflict with reality (i.e., we can detect liars and cheaters).

4. Dunbar (2003).

5. Steele, Ferrari, and Fogassi (2012); and Stout and Chaminade (2012).

6. Barham (2013). See also Ambrose (2010); and Wadley (2013).

7. Leacock (1969).

8. Howell (2010). The Ju/'hoansi are sometimes referred to as the !Kung or more generically as "Bushmen." They speak a "click language," and the / and ! refer to different kinds of clicks; the ' indicates what linguists call a glottal stop, a millisecond cessation of sound. Watch the silly movie *The Gods Must Be Crazy* and you can hear this language.

9. Altman (1987).

10. Stiner, Gopher, and Barkai (2011); Stiner (2013).

11. Henshilwood, d'Errico, and Watts (2009).

12. Texier et al. (2010).

13. For overview and references, see Stiner (2014). Interestingly, there are very few examples of "art" associated with Neanderthals in Europe (although it is debatable whether this is because Neanderthals did not do art or merely an issue of preservation). And a 500,000-year-old shell found during a nineteenth-century excavation in Indonesia might have a few intentional etchings on its surface; see Joordens et al.(2015).

14. Ambrose (2003).

15. Harpending and Rogers (2000); and Li and Durbin (2011). Note that this is a highly contested field with many confounding factors.

16. Lewis-Williams (2002).

17. Dennett (2006); Boyer (2001); Boyer and Bergstrom (2008); Atran (2002); and Dawkins (2006). Some scientists feel compelled to let the reader know they are atheists and that they came to that position through reason: if religion can be accounted for by evolution, then there's no need to add the divine. Maybe, but I've never been satisfied by that logic. By demonstrating that evolution can account for religion, we logically rule out divine intervention in the process, but we do not necessarily rule out the divine. I won't dwell on this subject except to say that I am not an atheist (full disclosure: I am a Bahá'í), but I do think the *capacity* for religion arose through natural selection.

18. Pettitt (2013).

19. Gargett et al. (1989); and Sommer (1999). This is also a highly controversial subject: see Zilhão (2015).

20. Smith (2004).
21. Wiessner (2002).

CHAPTER 5: BREAD AND BEER

1. See Shipman (2015) and Skoglund et al. (2015). Modern dogs are all descendants of an early, domesticated wolf-dog. We know this from both genetics and skull forms; however, since those early domesticated wolf-dogs could interbreed with wild wolves and coyotes, it is difficult to pinpoint when domesticated dogs first appeared.

2. Sheep and goats are domesticated in southwest Asia by 7000 B.C., and cows and oxen in southwest Asia and north Africa by the same time. Pigs are first domesticated in southwest Asia by 7000 B.C., and the horse in central Asia about 4000 B.C. However, it is very difficult to tell the difference between wild and domesticated animals from their bones. The bones of modern wild sheep and domesticated sheep, for example, are easy to distinguish, but the bones of the earliest sheep kept in captivity would have looked no different from those of wild sheep. Therefore, our earliest dates on domesticated animals most likely underestimate the age of domestication, perhaps by as much as one thousand years.

3. United Nations Food and Agriculture Organization statistics for 2013 (http://faostat3.fao.org/browse/Q/QC/E). Not all of this production goes to humans; a portion of maize, for example, is used as livestock feed and to produce ethanol for biofuels. And some is used to produce various alcoholic beverages.

4. He left a letter, with instructions that it not be opened for ten years. When it was opened in 1968, it didn't give an adequate explanation. He rarely used his first name, always publishing under V. Gordon Childe; for a biography of Childe, see Trigger (1980).

5. Childe (1936); for further evidence of his ability to synthesize archaeological data, see Childe (1942).

6. Skeletons had been found earlier in 1848 and 1826, but their significance was not recognized.

7. Genetic data have also been recovered from the molars of two adult males, but the highest coverage is from the young girl's finger. See Reich et al. (2010).

8. When humans arrived in North America is a hotly contested topic. The earliest definitive evidence, in my opinion, comes from the site of Paisley Five-Mile cave in Oregon—it consists of human coprolites, or desiccated human feces (based on DNA) that are some 14,500 years old. There are claims of an even older human presence on the East Coast, perhaps 20,000 or more years old, but again in my opinion, the evidence is not conclusive. For a readable overview of the New World colonization by the ancestors of Native Americans, see Meltzer (2009).

9. The only places without a human footprint at 10,000 B.C. would be occupied in the last few thousand years, places like the islands of Polynesia and Micronesia, starting about 2000 B.C.; both New Zealand and Hawaii in the last thousand years; Madagascar about 2000 B.C.; Iceland about A.D. 800; and Antarctica, which was not visited until the nineteenth century.

10. Simms (1987). A listing of return rates of many different kinds of hunted and gathered foods can be found in Kelly (2013b).

11. Anthropologists have studied how hunter-gatherers move using other models; see Kelly (2013b).

12. See Barker (2006) for a global overview of agricultural origins.

13. Until 2009, geologists placed the Pliocene/Pleistocene boundary at about 1.8 million years ago. New dates on the beginning of continental glaciation, however, changed the era's time range.

14. Such thick sheets of ice take on lives of their own and they move, gliding on a layer of water, squeezed out of the ice mass by its own tremendous weight. The ice sheets moved slowly, but powerfully enough to plow up huge piles of earth along their fronts—one of those piles is New York's Long Island. The vast bulk of ice even pressed some places, such as Scandinavia and the state of Maine, down into the planet; some of those places are still rebounding today, rising a few millimeters a year above the sea.

15. Zahid, Robinson, and Kelly (2016). This is the long-term rate; over the short term, population experienced higher and lower rates in response to changing climate conditions; see also Kelly et al. (2013).

16. Named after a flower, *Dryas octopetala,* that prefers cold environments; its pollen in sediment cores helped first chart the swift return to cold conditions. A previous short cold period about 14,000 years ago is labeled the Older Dryas.

17. This is referred to as "thermohaline circulation" and is a product of water temperature and salinity (and other variables such as wind). See Alley (2007); Broecker (2010); Muschitiello et al. (2015); Not and Hillaire-Marcel (2012).

18. True einkorn and emmer wheat are grown only for specialty markets today; the modern plants are descendants of hexaploid wheats that first evolved in those early farmers' fields through hybridization with other grasses.

19. Doebley (2004).

20. A focus on this aspect of plant and animal domestication falls under the theoretical area known as "niche construction theory" (see Smith 2015). Some propose it as an alternative to the optimal foraging model described in this chapter, but I see them as compatible. Humans modify their environment through intentional selection of, for example, large seeds, as well as through actions such as irrigation. Humans then respond to their new environment; the Diet Breadth Model tells us that increasing a plant's return rate allows that plant to leapfrog other potential foods in the diet. The result is a diet dominated by one or a few domesticated plants.

21. A trade language is a simple language that is used among groups who otherwise speak different languages. It is often a simplified version of one that incorporates elements of others. The Chinook trade language, sometimes called Chinook Jargon, is based on the Chinook language of the lower Columbia River with elements of other Northwest Coast languages.

22. In evolutionary theory this is known as "costly signaling." In the animal kingdom, such ostentatious displays are used to attract mates. The humongous, eye-catching tail of a peacock, for example, says to the peahens, "I can invest a

lot of my energy in this tail, and yet it does me no harm. I am powerful. Pick me." Similarly, competitive feasts are a way to find and cement alliances by demonstrating power through wasteful displays of wealth. For a discussion of feasting, see Hayden (2014).

23. Bocquet-Appel (2015).

24. Breast-feeding can require up to one thousand extra calories a day.

CHAPTER 6: KINGS AND CHAINS

1. Fagan (1975).

2. After you look at the Rosetta stone, turn to your right to see the massive black granite statue of Ramesses II, pillaged for the British government by Giovanni Battista Belzoni in 1815 and a source of inspiration for Shelley's poem *Ozymandias;* look to your left and you'll see my favorite objects in the museum, life-sized Egyptian statues of the lion-headed goddess Sekhmet, carved in black granite.

3. Roscoe (2009).

4. Lehner (1997). Sneferu's Red Pyramid has an exterior angle of just less than 44 degrees, a value clearly adopted from the lesson of the Bent Pyramid. Khufu's pyramid has an exterior angle of just less than 52 degrees, which is probably the maximum angle for safe stone-pyramid construction.

5. You've perhaps heard that the Inca fit massive stones together so tightly, and without the benefit of mortar, that you cannot slip the blade of a knife between them. Having visited Machu Picchu with a pocketknife, I can assure you this is true.

6. Metallurgy appeared at different times in other places in the world. Asia, for example, lacks a "Copper Age," and bronze tools appear in China about 2000 B.C., and not until 1250 B.C. throughout much of the rest of Southeast Asia and Japan. Iron tools appear throughout much of China and Southeast Asia about 500 B.C. There was virtually no metalworking in the New World, with the exception of some copper tools and ornaments (not smelted but fashioned from raw copper deposits) and gold and silver smelting in highland South America. Metals, largely copper and gold, did not appear until A.D. 600 in parts of Mexico and somewhat earlier in Central America.

7. For curious Americans, it's her son Prince Charles; his eldest son, Prince William; William's son, Prince George; William's daughter, Princess Charlotte; and then William's brother, Prince Henry. Royalphiles could tell you the next forty or so people in line.

8. Briggs (1970).

9. Fry (2007).

10. See Ames and Maschner (1999).

11. Kelly (2013a, 2013b). Population pressure was measured as a group's population density relative to a measure of that group's environment's productivity.

12. Such depression fractures are usually on the left side; because most people are right-handed, whacking someone on the head in hand-to-hand combat results in more cranial dents and fractures on the skull's left side.

13. See Wendorf (1968). There is a new case of extreme violence against a group at the site of Nataruk in Kenya dated to about 8000 B.C.; see Mirazón Lahr et al. (2016).

14. Haas and Piscitelli (2013).

15. Ferguson (2013).

16. See papers in Allen and Jones (2014).

17. The Bushmen quote is from Lee (1979: 246); the Kwakwaka'wakh quote is from Codere (1950: 120).

18. I remember first using these files in the 1970s. At that time, the files consisted of tens of thousands of 4″ × 6″ slips of paper, held in dozens of filing cabinets. If you wanted to know something about, say, marriage practices across different cultures, you went to the appropriate cabinet and pulled out all the pieces of paper under *marriage,* usually sustaining a number of paper cuts in the process. On each of these was a passage copied from an ethnography describing some aspect of that culture's marriage practices (sometimes there were quite a few pages). If you were curious about the relationship between marriage practices and subsistence, you could then pull out all the pieces of paper on food and compile your own data table, looking for patterns and correlations. I spent many, many hours in the library with these thousands of bits of paper. I'm happy to say that today these data are online and much easier to use.

19. Ember and Ember (1992); Ember, Adem, and Skoggard (2013).

20. Keith (2004) describes how World War I was fought by America's poor.

21. Atran (2010).

22. Flannery and Marcus (2012).

23. Anthropologists find that social inequality and gender inequality go hand in hand. As economic inequality between classes becomes greater, so too does the level of inequality between men and women.

CHAPTER 7: NOTHING LASTS FOREVER

1. The first successful trans-Atlantic cable was laid in 1858, though it only worked a few weeks; others were laid in the following decades.

2. A term coined by Dutch chemist Paul Crutzen; others have suggested the term *catastrophozoic.*

3. Steffen, Broadgate, et al. (2015); Steffen, Richardson, et al. (2015).

4. Developed in the late 1950s, microchips were not commercially viable until the 1980s.

5. Well into the nineteenth century the child mortality rate (i.e., before the age of fifteen) was 40–50 percent—little different from that of our prehistoric hunter-gatherer ancestors. This improved with the discovery of germ theory, anesthesia, and antiseptic operating rooms. And an understanding of disease helped improve living conditions and reduced mortality—for example, the realization that cholera did not result from "bad air" but from the dumping of human waste into rivers that supplied a population's drinking water. Likewise, the growing global food market and the industrialization of farming reduced mortality by increasing the abundance and security of the food supply.

6. The governments of Japan, Denmark, and France encourage couples to have more than one child, and some even provide subsidies; still Japan's population is expected to plummet by 50 percent over the next century. The cause of this decline has to do with the perceived cost of raising children, which in wealthy nations includes quality preschool and day care, extracurricular activities (sports, music, art), and a university education; increased involvement of women in the work force, which discourages large, baby-boomer-type families; and the availability of effective contraceptives.

7. Roser (2015).

8. Variously attributed to Yogi Berra, Casey Stengel, Mark Twain, and Niels Bohr, among others.

9. Kay, one of the creators of desktop computers, apparently said this in 1971 at a meeting of Xerox's Palo Alto Research Center. He was most likely paraphrasing the physicist Dennis Gabor who wrote in his 1963 book, *Inventing the Future*, "The future cannot be predicted, but futures can be invented." Both of them were referring to technology, however, not human organization.

10. Quoted in Ackerman (2014: 181).

11. Or films such as the Mad Max series, *Elysium, Blade Runner, Soylent Green, Planet of the Apes*—the list goes on. However, our vision of the future as bleak is a cultural fact; it's what we believe to be true. Once we understand that, we recognize our potential to create the future we want.

12. Micklethwait and Wooldridge (2014); for an earlier example, see Waltz (1954). For recent quantitative analyses see Peregrin, Ember, and Ember (2004); Carneiro (2004); Graber (2004); Roscoe (2004); Taagepera (1978).

13. Using simple linear regression, and then solving the resulting equation for X, population, when Y, the size of the largest country, is equivalent to 133 million square kilometers.

14. I am including Taiwan, a country that some others do not recognize.

15. This is what set the Luddites to smashing textile machinery in early nineteenth-century Britain. But they simply wanted to remain employed, not to give their name to anyone who opposed technological progress.

16. "Future of Jobs" (2014).

17. "Future of Jobs" (2014). This is largely so that employers can avoid the high cost of benefits mandated for full-time employees.

18. With the sale of Zenith to Korea in 1995, there were no longer any televisions produced in the United States. In 2012 Element Electronics began production in the United States, but nearly all televisions in American homes today are made overseas.

19. See Friedman (2005).

20. "A Sub-Saharan Scramble" (2015).

21. In 1944 the unit cost for a P-51 Mustang was about $51,000. My father, who served in the Pacific Theater during World War II, told me that if a Mustang broke a landing gear strut on the deck of an aircraft carrier, the pilot was yanked out and the plane shoved overboard because there were other planes, probably running on fumes, that needed to land—and Mustangs were considered expendable.

22. The Congressional Research Service placed the cost at $1.6 trillion; however, adding in other costs, such as increased veterans benefits, some economists place the cost at between $4 trillion and $6 trillion.

23. Over half the federal government's discretionary spending goes to defense, and military spending has increased by 50 percent since 9/11 while other spending has increased by only 13.5 percent (National Priorities Project, based on data from the Office of Management and Budget). The United States is now embarking on a trillion-dollar upgrade of its nuclear weapon capacity.

24. Fallows (2015).

25. Keegan (1993: 59). See also Goldstein (2012); and Human Security Report Project (2011).

26. Other places in the world that have talked secession or that have achieved partial recognition of autonomous status include Transnistria, South Ossetia, Abkhazia, Somaliland, West Papua New Guinea, and South Tyrol.

27. Armstrong (2014).

28. Barber (1996).

29. The Tea Party claims the United States has a special status in the world, captured by the phrase "American exceptionalism." This phrase was first used, and disparagingly at that, by Joseph Stalin, in reference to the American Communist Party's assertion that no violent revolution would be needed for the conversion of the United States. America *is* an exceptional country, just like every other one. Claiming that we don't have to play by the rules is no different than the largest, wealthiest kid on the street claiming that everyone must play by his rules because "it's my ball." Such an attitude is not conducive to peaceful relations among schoolyard children or among nations.

30. And another effect, prevalent among the powerless, is an increased suicide rate, something that we sadly see among many "tribal" indigenous people. See Lyons (2015).

31. In fact, the historian Akira Iriye (2002) has done exactly that. The grand story of the twentieth century is the development of international organizations and an increasingly international web of connections at all levels, economic, governmental, and cultural.

32. One outcome could be a few large cooperative units (maybe we should call them "superstates") that viciously compete with one another, such as the United States–Canada–Latin America–European Union versus Russia–the Near East–China–India (Graber 2004). But this wouldn't be my preference.

33. Cartwright (2008: 49). We saw this happen in the Middle East during the so-called Arab Spring, where Facebook and Twitter were the tools of dramatic change. National boundaries mean little to social media.

34. Khanna (2011). Davidson and Rees-Mogg (1997) see this taking place at the level of the individual. In the plugged-in information age, individuals can become free agents and sell their labor in a world marketplace.

35. Khanna (2013: SR5).

36. "Plan to Protect Refuge Has Alaskans Offended and Fearful over Money" (2015).

37. Quoted in "Sovereign State," *Wikipedia,* http://en.wikipedia.org/wiki/Sovereign_state, accessed 1/13/2015.

38. And often futile: you can build a wall around Miami, but water will simply seep up through the porous limestone on which it sits.

39. See Hsiang et al. (2011, 2013).

40. Kennedy (2006); Goldstein (2012).

41. As Ewing notes (2007: 35), the United Nation's 2004 Anand Report stated that the Security Council had to become more "pro-active" as well as "credible, legitimate and representative." It has so far failed to do so.

42. The complete quote, from *Innocents Abroad*, is "Travel is fatal to prejudice, bigotry, and narrow-mindedness, and many of our people need it sorely on these accounts. Broad, wholesome, charitable views of men and things cannot be acquired by vegetating in one little corner of the earth all one's lifetime." This is the best justification for a university to ensure that all students spend time abroad as part of their college education.

43. I admit there is downside: a desire to get movies to a potential audience of one billion leads producers to bow to the wishes of China's State General Administration of Press, Publication, Radio, Film, and Television. For example, the version of *Ironman III* that I saw in Shanghai had a different ending than that shown to American audiences, one that was blatant Chinese propaganda.

44. There are two basic political approaches to change: top down and bottom up. Much of our political debate revolves around which of these is best. Those favoring top-down approaches want, for example, more government social programs, universal health care, and an increase in the minimum wage or a guaranteed basic minimal income. They want to legislate the change they wish to see. The fear, of course, is that such a welfare state creates a culture of dependency, with a small elite supporting many "lazy" people.

Those favoring bottom-up approaches want market control, greater privatization, individual responsibility, and fewer regulations. They want to release constraints so that change happens "naturally," that is, from the bottom up. The fear about this structure is that it allows markets, governed by a profit motive and not social responsibility, to drive wages down and to wreak environmental and social havoc (e.g., by profiting from environmental destruction and exploitative wages).

Matt Ridley (2015), a libertarian, argues for the long-term efficacy of bottom-up approaches. But I think his analysis is flawed. First, there are cases where top-down approaches have done "good" things. The U.S. interstate highway system, defense, civil rights, and school integration are the sorts of things that are best done top down; without federal intervention we might still have governors standing in front of schoolhouse doors claiming, "Segregation forever." Second, Ridley assumes that top-down approaches are antievolutionary, but in fact, elite control of the social and economic structure evolves "naturally;" top-down approaches (including liberal democracies but also dictatorships) are a result of evolutionary processes.

The answer lies between the two. Dean Baker (2011), for example, argues for top-down approaches that create the sort of bottom-up behaviors that produce the greatest good for the greatest number.

Bibliography

Ackerman, Diane. 2014. *The Human Age: The World Shaped by Us.* Norton, New York.

Aiello, Leslie C., and Wheeler, Peter. 1995. "The Expensive-Tissue Hypothesis: The Brain and the Digestive System in Human and Primate Evolution." *Current Anthropology* 36: 199–221.

Allen, Mark, and Terry Jones, eds. 2014. *Violence and Warfare among Hunter-Gatherers.* Left Coast Press, Walnut Creek, CA.

Alley, Richard B. 2007. "Wally Was Right: Predictive Ability of the North Atlantic 'Conveyor Belt' Hypothesis for Abrupt Climate Change." *Annual Review of Earth and Planetary Sciences* 35: 241–272.

Altman, Jon C. 1987. *Hunter-Gatherers Today.* Australian Institute of Aboriginal Studies, Canberra.

Ambrose, Stanley H. 2003. "Did the Super-Eruption of Toba Cause a Human Population Bottleneck? Reply to Gathorne-Hardy and Harcourt-Smith." *Journal of Human Evolution* 45: 231–237.

———. 2010. "Coevolution of Composite-Tool Technology, Constructive Memory, and Language: Implications for the Evolution of Modern Human Behavior." *Current Anthropology* 51: S135–S147.

Ames, Kenneth, and Herbert D. G. Maschner. 1999. *Peoples of the Northwest Coast: Their Archaeology and Prehistory.* Thames and Hudson, London.

Antón, Susan. 2003. "A Natural History of *Homo erectus.*" *Yearbook of Physical Anthropology* 46: 126–170.

Armstrong, Karen. 2014. *Fields of Blood: Religion and the History of Violence.* Knopf, New York.

Atran, Scott. 2002. *In Gods We Trust: The Evolutionary Landscape of Religion.* Oxford University Press, Oxford.

———. 2010. *Talking to the Enemy: Faith, Brotherhood, and the Unmaking of Terrorists*. HarperCollins, New York.

Baker, Dean. 2011. *The End of Loser Liberalism*. Center for Economic and Policy Research, Washington, DC.

Barber, Benjamin. 1996. *Jihad versus McWorld*. Ballantine, New York.

Barham, Lawrence. 2013. *From Hand to Handle: The First Industrial Revolution*. Oxford University Press, Oxford.

Barker, Graeme. 2006. *The Agricultural Revolution in Prehistory*. Oxford University Press, Oxford.

Berna, F. Francesco, Paul Goldberg, Liora Kolska Horwitz, James Brink, Sharon Holt, Marion Bamford, and Michael Chazan. 2012. "Microstratigraphic Evidence of In Situ Fire in the Acheulean Strata of Wonderwerk Cave, Northern Cape Province, South Africa." *Proceedings of the National Academy of Sciences* 109: E1215–E1220.

Bocquet-Appel, Jean-Pierre. 2015. "When the World's Population Took Off: The Springboard of the Neolithic Demographic Transition." *Science* 333: 560–561.

Boggs, Carl. 2000. *The End of Politics: Corporate Power and the Decline of the Public Sphere*. Guilford Press, New York.

Boyer, Pascal. 2001. *Religion Explained: The Evolutionary Origins of Religious Thought*. Basic Books, New York.

Boyer, Pascal, and Brian Bergstrom. 2008. "Evolutionary Perspectives on Religion." *Annual Review of Anthropology* 37: 111–130.

Brauer, Günter. 2014. "Origin of Modern Humans." In *Handbook of Paleoanthropology*, 2nd ed., edited by Winfried Henke and Ian Tattersall, 2300–2331. Springer, Heidelberg.

Briggs, Jean. 1970. *Never in Anger: Portrait of an Eskimo Family*. Harvard University Press, Cambridge.

Broecker, Wallace S. 2010. *The Great Ocean Conveyor: Discovering the Trigger for Abrupt Climate Change*. Princeton University Press, Princeton.

Carneiro, Robert. 2004. "The Political Unification of the World: Whether, When, and How—Some Speculations." *Cross-Cultural Research* 38: 162–177.

Carswell, Douglas. 2012. *The End of Politics*. Biteback Publishing, London.

Cartwright, James. 2008. "Deciphering the Mega-Trends." In *The Way We Will Be 50 Years from Today: 60 of the World's Greatest Minds Share Their Visions of the Next Half Century*, edited by Mike Wallace, 46–51. Thomas Nelson, Nashville.

Childe, V. Gordon. 1936. *Man Makes Himself*. Watts, London.

———. 1942. *What Happened in History?* Penguin, Harmondsworth.

Clover, Charles. 2004. *The End of the Line*. New Press, New York.

Codere, Helen. 1950. *Fighting with Property: A Study of Kwakiutl Potlatching and Warfare, 1792–1930*. American Ethnological Society Monograph 18. University of Washington Press, Seattle.

Cronk, Lee, and B.L. Leech. 2013. *Meeting at Grand Central: Understanding the Social and Evolutionary Roots of Cooperation*. Princeton University Press, Princeton, NJ.

Davidson, James Dale, and Lord William Rees-Mogg. 1997. *The Sovereign Individual: Mastering the Transition to the Information Age*. Touchstone, New York.

Dawkins, Richard. 2006. *The God Delusion*. Houghton Mifflin, Boston.

Deaton, Angus. 2013. *The Great Escape: Health, Wealth and the Origins of Inequality*. Princeton University Press, Princeton, NJ.

Dennett, Daniel. 2006. *Breaking the Spell: Religion as a Natural Phenomenon*. Viking, New York.

Diamond, Jared. 2012. *The World until Yesterday: What We Can Learn from Traditional Societies*. Penguin, New York.

Doebley, John. 2004. "The Genetics of Maize Evolution." *Annual Review of Genetics* 38:37–59.

D'Souza, Dinesh. 1996. *The End of Racism*. Free Press, New York.

Dunbar, Robin I. M. 2003. "The Social Brain: Mind, Language, and Society in Evolutionary Perspective." *Annual Review of Anthropology* 32: 163–181.

Ember, Carol, and Melvin Ember. 1992. "Resource Unpredictability, Mistrust, and War: A Cross-Cultural Study." *Journal of Conflict Resolution* 36: 242–262.

Ember, Carol R., Teferi Abate Adem, and Ian Skoggard. 2013. "Risk, Uncertainty, and Violence in Eastern Africa: A Regional Comparison." *Human Nature* 24: 33–58.

Ewing, Sovaida Ma'ani. 2007. *Collective Security within Reach*. George Ronald, Oxford.

Fagan, Brian. 1975. *The Rape of the Nile*. Scribner's, New York.

Fallows, James. 2015. "Why Do the Best Soldiers in the World Keep Losing?" *Atlantic* (January/February).

Ferguson, Brian. 2013. "Pinker's List: Exaggerating Prehistoric War Mortality." In *War, Peace, and Human Nature: The Convergence of Evolutionary and Cultural Views*, edited by Douglas Fry, 112–131. Oxford University Press, Oxford.

Ferraro, Joseph V., Thomas W. Plummer Briana L. Pobiner, James S. Oliver, Laura C. Bishop, David R. Braun, Peter W. Ditchfield, John W. Seaman III, Katie M. Binetti, John W. Seaman Jr., Fritz Hertel, and Richard Potts. 2013. "Earliest Archaeological Evidence of Persistent Hominin Carnivory." *Plos One*. doi.org/10.1371/journal.pone.0062174.

Ferring, Reid, Oriol Oms, Jordi Agustí, Francesco Berna, Medea Nioradze, Teona Shelia, Martha Tappen, Abesalom Vekua, David Zhvania, and David Lordkipanidze. 2011. "Earliest Human Occupations at Dmanisi (Georgian Caucasus) dated to 1.85–1.78 Ma." *Proceedings of the National Academy of Sciences* 108: 10432–10436.

Flannery, Kent, and Joyce Marcus. 2012. *The Creation of Inequality*. Harvard University Press, Cambridge, MA.

Fleckinger, Angelika. 2003. *Ötzi, the Iceman*. 3rd ed. Folio, Rome.

Fowler, Brenda. 2000. *Iceman: Uncovering the Life and Times of a Prehistoric Man Found in an Alpine Glacier*. University of Chicago Press, Chicago.

Friedman, Thomas. 2005. *The World Is Flat*. Farrar, Straus & Giroux, New York.

Fry, Douglas. 2007. *Beyond War: The Human Potential for Peace.* Oxford University Press, Oxford.

Fukuyama, Francis. 1992. *The End of History and The Last Man.* Free Press, New York.

"The Future of Jobs: The Onrushing Wave." 2014. *Economist,* January 18.

Gargett, Robert H., Harvey M. Bricker, Geoffrey Clark, John Lindly, Catherine Farizy, Claude Masset, David W. Frayer, Anta Montet-White, Clive Gamble, Antonio Gilman, Arlette Leroi-Gourhan, M.I. Martínez Navarrete, Paul Ossa, Erik Trinkaus, and Andrzej W. Weber. 1989. "Grave Shortcomings: The Evidence for Neandertal Burial." *Current Anthropology* 30: 157–190.

Goldstein, Joshua. 2012. *Winning the War on War: The Decline of Armed Conflict Worldwide.* Penguin, New York.

Gore, Al. 2013. *The Future: Six Drivers of Global Change.* Random House, New York.

Gowlett, John A.J., and Richard Wrangham. 2013. Earliest Fire in Africa: Towards the Convergence of Archaeological Evidence and the Cooking Hypothesis. *Azania: Archaeological Research in Africa* 48: 5–30.

Graber, Robert. 2004. "Is a World State Just a Matter of Time? A Population-Pressure Alternative." *Cross-Cultural Research* 38: 147–161.

Greco, Thomas. 2009. *The End of Money and the Future of Civilization.* Chelsea Green Publishers, White River Junction, VT.

Haas, Jonathan, and Matthew Piscitelli. 2013. "The Prehistory of Warfare: Misled by Ethnography." In *War, Peace, and Human Nature: The Convergence of Evolutionary and Cultural Views,* edited by Douglas Fry, 168–190. Oxford University Press, Oxford.

Hardoon, Deborah, Sophia Ayele, and Ricardo Fuentes-Nieva. 2016. "An Economy for the 1%." Oxfam Briefing Paper 210 (January 18). https://www.oxfam.org/sites/www.oxfam.org/files/file_attachments/bp210-economy-one-percent-tax-havens-180116-en_0.pdf.

Harmand, Sonia, Jason E. Lewis, Craig S. Feibel, Christopher J. Lepre, Sandrine Prat, Arnaud Lenoble, Xavier Boës, Rhonda L. Quinn, Michel Brenet, Adrian Arroyo, Nicholas Taylor, Sophie Clément, Guillaume Daver, Jean-Philip Brugal, Louise Leakey, Richard A. Mortlock, James D. Wright, Sammy Lokorodi, Christopher Kirwa, Dennis V. Kent, and Hélène Roche. 2015. "3.3-Million-Year-Old Stone Tools from Lomekwi 3, West Turkana, Kenya." *Nature* 521: 310–315.

Harpending, Henry, and Alan Rogers. 2000. "Genetic Perspectives on Human Origins and Differentiation." *Annual Review of Genomics and Human Genetics* 1: 361–385.

Harris, Sam. 2004. *The End of Faith.* Norton., New York.

Hauser, Kitty. 2008. *Bloody Old Britain: O.G.S. Crawford and the Archaeology of Modern Life.* Granta Books, London.

Hayden, Brian. 2014. *The Power of Feasts: From Prehistory to the Present.* Cambridge University Press, Cambridge.

Heinberg, Richard. 2011. *The End of Growth.* New Society Publishers, Gabriola, British Columbia.

Henshilwood, C. S., Fransesco d'Errico, and Ian Watts. 2009. "Engraved Ochres from the Middle Stone Age Levels at Blombos Cave, South Africa." *Journal of Human Evolution* 57: 27–47.

Horgan, John. 1996. *The End of Science.* Addison-Wesley, Boston.

———. 2012. *The End of War.* McSweeney's Books, San Francisco.

Howell, Nancy. 2010. *Life Histories of the Dobe !Kung: Food, Fatness, and Well-Being over the Life-Span.* University of California Press, Berkeley.

Hsiang, Solomon M., Marshall Burke, and Edward Miguel. 2013. "Quantifying the Influence of Climate on Human Conflict." *Science* 341. doi:1235367-1–1235367-14.

Hsiang, Solomon M., Kyle C. Meng, and Mark A. Cane. 2011. "Civil Conflicts Are Associated with the Global Climate." *Nature* 476: 438–441.

Human Security Report Project. 2011. *Human Security Report 2009/2010: The Causes of Peace and the Shrinking Costs of War.* Oxford University Press, Oxford.

Iriye, Akira. 2002. *Global Community: The Role of International Organizations in the Making of the Contemporary World.* University of California Press, Berkeley.

Joordens, Josephine C., Francesco d'Errico, Frank P. Wesselingh, Stephen Munro, John de Vos, Jakob Wallinga, Christina Ankjærgaard, Tony Reimann, Jan R. Wijbrans, Klaudia F. Kuiper, Herman J. Mücher, Hélène Coqueugniot, Vincent Prié, Ineke Joosten, Bertil van Os, Anne S. Schulp, Michel Panuel, Victoria van der Haas, Wim Lustenhouwer, John J. G. Reijmer, and Wil Roebroeks. 2015. "*Homo erectus* at Trinil on Java Used Shells for Tool Production and Engraving." *Nature* 518: 228–231.

Kaminski, Juliane. 2014. "Theory of Mind: A Primatological Perspective." In *Handbook of Paleoanthropology*, 2nd ed., edited by Winfried Henke and Ian Tattersall, 1741–1757. Springer, Heidelberg.

Kaplan, Robert. 1996. *The Ends of the Earth: From Togo to Turkmenistan, from Iran to Cambodia, a Journey to the Frontiers of Anarchy.* Vintage, New York.

Keegan, John. 1993. *A History of Warfare.* Vintage, New York.

Keith, Jeanette. 2004. *Rich Man's War, Poor Man's Fight.* University of North Carolina Press, Chapel Hill.

Kelly, Robert K., Todd Surovell, Bryan Shuman, and Geoff Smith. 2013. "A Continuous Climatic Impact on Holocene Human Population in the Rocky Mountains." *Proceedings of the National Academy of Sciences* 110: 443–447.

Kelly, Robert L. 2013a. "From the Peaceful to the Warlike: Ethnographic and Archaeological Insights into Hunter-Gatherer Warfare and Homicide." In *War, Peace, and Human Nature: The Convergence of Evolutionary and Cultural Views*, edited by Douglas Fry, 151–167. Oxford University Press, Oxford.

———. 2013b. *The Lifeways of Hunter-Gatherers: The Foraging Spectrum.* 2nd ed. Cambridge University Press, Cambridge.

Kennedy, Paul. 2006. *The Parliament of Man: The Past, Present and Future of the United Nations.* Vintage, New York.

Kenny, Charles. 2012. *Getting Better: Why Global Development Is Succeeding and How We Can Improve the World Even More.* Basic Books, New York.

Kessler, David. 2009. *The End of Overeating.* Rodale, New York.

Khanna, Parag. 2011. *How to Run the World: Charting a Course to the Next Renaissance.* Random House, New York.

———. 2013. "The End of the Nation-State?" *New York Times,* Sunday, October 12, SR5.

Kissinger, Henry. 2014. *World Order.* Penguin Books, New York.

Klein, Naomi. 2015. *This Changes Everything: Capitalism versus the Climate.* Simon & Schuster, New York.

Kolbert, Elizabeth. 2014. *The Sixth Extinction: An Unnatural History.* Henry Holt, New York.

Leacock, Eleanor. 1969. "The Montagnais-Naskapi Band." In Contributions to Anthropology: Band Societies, edited by D. Damas, 1–17. *National Museum of Canada Bulletin* 228. National Museum of Canada, Ottawa.

Lee, Richard. 1979. *The !Kung San: Men, Women, and Work in a Foraging Society.* Cambridge University Press, Cambridge.

———. 1980. "Lactation, Ovulation, Infanticide, and Women's Work: A Study of Hunter-Gatherer Population." In *Biosocial Mechanisms of Population Regulation,* edited by M. Cohen, R. Malpass, and H. Klein, 321–348. Yale University Press, New Haven.

Lehner, Mark. 1997. *The Complete Pyramids.* Thames and Hudson, London.

Lewis-Williams, David. 2002. *The Mind in the Cave.* Thames and Hudson, London.

Li, Heng, and Richard Durbin. 2011. "Inference of Human Population History from Individual Whole-Genome Sequences." *Nature* 475: 493–496.

Lordkipanidze, D., Marcia S. Ponce de León, Ann Margvelashvili, Yoel Rak, G. Philip Rightmire, Abesalom Vekua, and Christoph P. E. Zollikofer. 2013. "A Complete Skull from Dmanisi, Georgia, and the Evolutionary Biology of Early *Homo.*" *Science* 342: 326–331.

Lovejoy, C. O. 1988. "Evolution of Human Walking." *Scientific American* 259: 82–89.

Lyons, Charles. 2015. "Suicide Spreads through a Brazilian Tribe," *New York Times,* January 4, SR6.

Marks, Jonathan. 2002. *What It Means to Be 98% Chimpanzee.* University of California Press, Berkeley.

McKibben, Bill. 1989. *The End of Nature.* Anchor, New York.

Meltzer, David. 2009. *First Peoples in a New World: Colonizing Ice Age America.* University of California Press, Berkeley.

Micklethwait, John, and Adrian Wooldridge. 2014. *The Fourth Revolution: The Global Race to Reinvent the State.* Penguin, New York.

Mirazón Lahr, M., F. Rivera, R. K. Power, A. Mounier, B. Copsey, F. Crivellaro, J. E. Edung, J. M. Maillo Fernandez, C. Kiarie, J. Lawrence, A. Leakey, E. Mbua, H. Miller, A. Muigai, D. M. Mukhongo, A. Van Baelen, R. Wood, J.-L. Schwenninger, R. Grün, H. Achyuthan, A. Wilshaw, and R. A. Foley. 2016. "Inter-Group Violence among Early Holocene Hunter-Gatherers of West Turkana, Kenya." *Nature* 529: 394–398.

Mithen, Steven. 1996. *The Prehistory of the Mind.* Thames and Hudson, London.

Moura, A. C. de A., and P. C. Lee. 2004. "Capuchin Stone Tool Use in Caatinga Dry Forest." *Science* 306: 1909.

Muschitiello, Francesco, Francesco S. R. Pausata, Jenny E. Watson, Rienk H. Smittenberg, Abubakr A. M. Salih, Stephen J. Brooks, Nicola J. Whitehouse, Artemis Karlatou-Charalampopoulou, and Barbara Wohlfarth. 2015. "Fennoscandian Freshwater Control on Greenland Hydroclimate Shifts at the Onset of the Younger Dryas." *Nature Communications* 6: 8939. doi:10.1038/ncomms9939.

Napier, John. 1970. *The Roots of Mankind.* Smithsonian Books, Washington DC.

Not, Christelle, and Claude Hillaire-Marcel. 2012. "Enhanced Sea-Ice Export from the Arctic during the Younger Dryas." *Nature Communications* 3: 647. doi:10.1038/ncomms1658.

Oreskes, Naomi, and Erik M. Conway. 2014. *The Collapse of Western Civilization: A View from the Future.* Columbia University Press, New York.

Peregrin, Peter, Melvin Ember, and Carol Ember. 2004. "Predicting the Future State of the World Using Archaeological Data: An Exercise in Archaeomancy." *Cross-Cultural Research* 38: 133–146.

Pettitt, Paul. 2013. *The Paleolithic Origins of Human Burial.* Routledge, New York.

Pinker, Steven. 2012. *The Better Angels of Our Nature: Why Violence Has Declined.* Penguin, New York.

"Plan to Protect Refuge Has Alaskans Offended and Fearful Over Money." 2015. *New York Times*, January 26, A14.

Postman, Neil. 1995. *The End of Education.* Knopf, New York.

Rathje, William, and Cullen Murphy. 2001. *Rubbish! The Archaeology of Garbage.* University of Arizona Press, Tucson.

Reich, David, Richard E. Green, Martin Kircher, Johannes Krause, Nick Patterson, Eric Y. Durand, Bence Viola, Adrian W. Briggs, Udo Stenzel, Philip L. F. Johnson, Tomislav Maricic, Jeffrey M. Good, Tomas Marques-Bonet, Can Alkan, Qiaomei Fu, Swapan Mallick, Heng Li, Matthias Meyer, Evan E. Eichler, Mark Stoneking, Michael Richards, Sahra Talamo, Michael V. Shunkov, Anatoli P. Derevianko, and Jean-Jacques Hublin. 2010. "Genetic History of an Archaic Hominin Group from Denisova Cave in Siberia." Nature 468: 1053–1060.

Ridley, Matt. 2010. *The Rational Optimist: How Prosperity Evolves.* HarperCollins, New York.

———. 2015. *The Evolution of Everything.* HarperCollins, New York.

Rifkin, Jeremy. 1995. *The End of Work.* Putnam, New York.

Roberts, Paul. 2004. *The End of Oil.* Mariner Books, New York.

———. 2008. *The End of Food.* Houghton Mifflin, Boston.

Rodman, Peter S., and Henry M. McHenry. 1980. "Bioenergetics and the Origin of Hominid Bipedalism." *American Journal of Physical Anthropology* 52: 103–6.

Roebroeks, Wil, and Paola Villa. 2011. "On the Earliest Evidence for Habitual Use of Fire in Europe." *Proceedings of the National Academy of Sciences* 108: 5209–5214.

Roscoe, Paul. 2004. "The Problem with Polities: Some Problems in Forecasting Global Political Integration. *Cross-Cultural Research* 38: 102–118.

———. 2009. "Social Signaling and the Organization of Small-Scale Society: The Case of Contact-Era New Guinea." *Journal of Archaeological Method and Theory* 16: 69–116.

Roser, Max. 2015. "World Population Growth." OurWorldInData.org. http://ourworldindata.org/data/population-growth-vital-statistics/world-population-growth, retrieved February 13, 2016.

Rosin, Hanna. 2012. *The End of Men*. Riverhead Books, New York.

Sachs, Jeffrey. 2005. *The End of Poverty*. Penguin, New York.

Shipman, Pat. 2015. *The Invaders: How Humans and Their Dogs Drove Neanderthals to Extinction*. Harvard University Press, Cambridge, MA.

Simms, Steven. 1987. *Behavioral Ecology and Hunter-Gatherer Foraging: An Example from the Great Basin*. International Series 381. British Archaeological Reports, Oxford.

Skoglund, Pontus, Erik Ersmark, Eleftheria Palkopoulou, and Love Dale. 2015. "Ancient Wolf Genome Reveals an Early Divergence of Domestic Dog Ancestors and Admixture into High-Latitude Breeds." *Current Biology* 25:1515–1519.

Smith, Bruce D. 2015. "A Comparison of Niche Construction Theory and Diet Breadth Models as Explanatory Frameworks for the Initial Domestication of Plants and Animals." *Journal of Archaeological Research* 23: 215–262.

Smith, Eric. 2004. "Why Do Good Hunters Have Higher Reproductive Success?" *Human Nature* 15: 343–364.

Sommer, Jeffrey. 1999. "The Shanidar IV 'Flower Burial': An Evaluation of Neanderthal Burial Ritual." *Cambridge Archaeological Journal* 9: 127–137.

Steele, James, Pier Francesco Ferrari, and Leonardo Fogassi. 2012. "From Action to Language: Comparative Perspectives on Primate Tool Use, Gesture and the Evolution of Human Language." *Philosophical Transactions of the Royal Society B* 367: 4–9.

Steffen, Will, Wendy Broadgate, Lisa Deutsch, Owen Gaffney, and Cornelia Ludwig. 2015. "The Trajectory of the Anthropocene: The Great Acceleration." *The Anthropocene Review* 2(1): 81–98.

Steffen, Will, Katherine Richardson, Johan Rockström, Sarah E. Cornell, Ingo Fetzer, Elena M. Bennett, Reinette Biggs, Stephen R. Carpenter, Wim de Vries, Cynthia A. de Wit, Carl Folke, Dieter Gerten, Jens Heinke, Georgina M. Mace, Linn M. Persson, Veerabhadran Ramanathan, Belinda Reyers, and Sverker Sörlin. 2015. "Planetary Boundaries: Guiding Human Development on a Changing Planet." *Science* 347. doi:1259855-1-1259855-10.

Stiner, Mary. 2013. "An Unshakable Middle Paleolithic? Trends versus Conservatism in the Predatory Niche and Their Social Ramifications." *Current Anthropology* 54(S8): S288-S304.

———. 2014. "Finding a Common Band-Width: Causes of Convergence and Diversity in Paleolithic Beads." *Biological Theory* 9: 51–64.

Stiner, Mary, Avi Gopher, and Ran Barkai. 2011. "Hearth-Side Socioeconomics, Hunting and Paleoecology during the Late Lower Paleolithic at Qesem Cave, Israel." *Journal of Human Evolution* 60: 213–233.

Stout, Dietrich, and Thierry Chaminade. 2012. "Stone Tools, Language and the Brain in Human Evolution." *Philosophical Transactions of the Royal Society B* 367: 75–87.

Stringer, Christopher. 2014. "Why We Are Not All Multiregionalists Now." *Trends in Ecology and Evolution* 29: 248–251.

"A Sub-Saharan Scramble." 2015. *Economist,* January 24.

Suskind, Richard. 2008. *The End of Lawyers?* Oxford University Press, Oxford.

Taagepera, Rein. 1978. "Size and Duration of Empires: Systematics of Size." *Social Science Research* 7: 108–127.

Texier, Pierre-Jean, Guillaume Porraz, John Parkington, Jean-Philippe Rigaud, Cedric Poggenpoel, Christopher Miller, Chantal Tribolo, Caroline Cartwright, Aude Coudenneau, Richard Klein, Teresa Steele, and Christine Verna. 2010. "A Howiesons Poort Tradition of Engraving Ostrich Eggshell Containers Dated to 60,000 Years Ago at Diepkloof Rock Shelter, South Africa." *Proceedings of the National Academy of Sciences* 107: 6180–6185.

Thieme, Hartmut. 1997. "Lower Palaeolithic Hunting Spears from Germany." *Nature* 385: 807–810.

Trigger, Bruce. 1980. *Gordon Childe: Revolutions in Archaeology.* Thames and Hudson, London.

Toth, Nicholas, and Kathy Schick. 2009. "The Oldowan: The Tool Making of Early Hominins and Chimpanzees Compared." *Annual Review of Anthropology* 38: 289–305.

Twain, Mark. 1869. "Conclusion" in *Innocents Abroad.* Available online from Project Gutenberg, https://www.gutenberg.org/files/3176/3176-h/3176-h.htm #CONCLUSION.

Ungar, Peter. 2004. "Dental Topography and Diets of *Australopithecus afarensis* and Early *Homo." Journal of Human Evolution* 46: 605–622.

———. 2012. "Dental Evidence for the Reconstruction of Diet in African Early *Homo." Current Anthropology* 53(S6): S318-S329.

Vaughan, Christopher L. 2003. "Theories of Bipedal Walking: An Odyssey." Journal of Biomechanics 36: 513–523.

Vince, Gaia. 2014. *Adventures in the Anthropocene: A Journey to the Heart of the Planet We Made.* Chatto & Windus, London.

Wadley, Lyn. 2013. "Recognizing Complex Cognition through Innovative Technology in Stone Age and Palaeolithic Sites." *Cambridge Archaeological Journal* 23: 163–183.

Walker, Alan, and Richard Leakey. 1993. *The Nariokotome* Homo erectus *Skeleton.* Harvard University Press, Cambridge.

Waltz, Kenneth. 1954. *Man, the State, and War: A Theoretical Analysis.* Columbia University Press, New York.

Weisman, Alan. 2014. *Countdown.* Little, Brown, New York.

Wendorf, Fred. 1968. "Site 117: A Nubian Final Paleolithic Graveyard near Jebel Sahaba, Sudan." In *The Prehistory of Nubia,* edited by F. Wendorf, 954–987. Southern Methodist University Press, Dallas.

Wiessner, Polly. 2002. "Hunting, Healing, and Hxaro Exchange: A Long-Term Perspective on !Kung (Ju/'hoansi) Large-Game Hunting." *Evolution and Human Behavior* 23:407–36.

Wilson, E. O. 2002. *The Social Conquest of Earth.* Vintage, New York.

———. 2012. *The Future of Life.* Liveright, New York.

———. 2014. *The Meaning of Human Existence.* Liveright, New York.

Wolman, David. 2012. *The End of Money.* Da Capo Press, Boston.

Wrangham, Richard W. 2009. *Catching Fire: How Cooking Made Us Human.* Harvard University Press, Cambridge.

Wright, Robert. 2000. *Non-Zero: The Logic of Human Destiny.* Vintage, New York.

Zahid, H. Jabran, Erick Robinson, and Robert L. Kelly. 2016. "Agriculture, Population Growth and Statistical Analysis of the Radiocarbon Record." *Proceedings of the National Academy of Sciences* 113: 931–935.

Zilhão, João. 2015. "Lower and Middle Paleolithic Behaviours and the Origins of Ritual Burial." In *Death Rituals, Social Order and the Archaeology of Immortality in the Ancient World,* edited by Colin Renfrew, Michael J. Boyd, and Iain Morley, 27–44. Cambridge University Press, Cambridge.

Zink, Katherine D., and Daniel E. Lieberman. 2016. "Impact of Meat and Lower Palaeolithic Food Processing Techniques on Chewing in Humans." *Nature* 531: 500–503.

Index